Significant Cities

Frances Dean

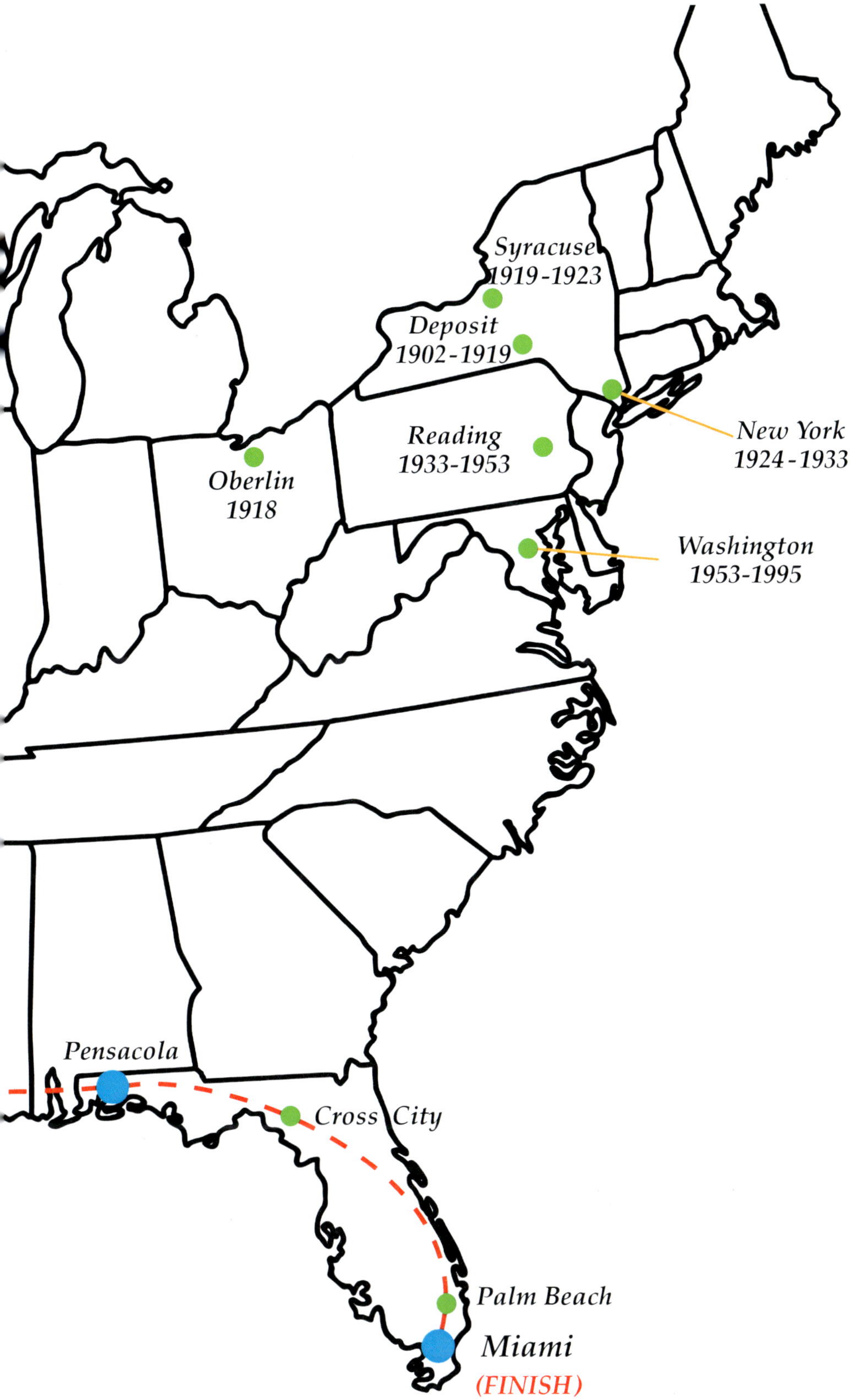

She Looked to the Sky

Punches Run tower, in the Nolde Forest, Pennsylvania

She Looked to the Sky

The Remarkable Life of a Pioneer Aviator

by

Frances Dean Nolde

Hugh Fortmiller, Editor

Boxborough, Massachusetts

2022

DEDICATION

To the women of the world, my sisters,
who don't realize they have a purpose until they find it.

ISBN: 979-8-218-04868-6

A full list of photographs and images appear on page 198. Photo and other credits: Family photographs, newspaper and magazine photographs, and news copy and other images come from the author's files, or the files of Frances Dean Wilcox Nolde. When available, dates, names of photographers, and publications are given; in most cases, credits cannot be found. Some photographs and images come from the internet. Many photographs are courtesy of Nolde Forest Environmental Education Center, Brent M. Erb, Director. Reproduction of a painting by Donald Collins, courtesy of the Civil Air Patrol: National Headquarters, Maxwell AFB, AL.

When NBC did not claim rights to the script from "Gloria Gay's Affairs," Larry Groebe, Founder of the Generic Radio Workshop in Dallas, Texas, recommended that a portion of the script be included as "fair use."

BOOK DESIGN BY JEANNE ABBOUD

PRINTING CONSULTANT: DAVID B. LIVESEY

PRINTED IN THE UNITED STATES

Contents

FOR THE READER

Whose Story?

She Looked to the Sky is both biography and memoir, a biography of my mother and a memoir of how her behavior and values affected my growing up. For those who prefer one genre or the other, I ask for your indulgence to let the two intermingle.

I address my parents as they themselves chose to be known. For their children, my mother chose "Mother." My father chose "Daddy." The contrast between the two selections indicates who was in charge. For their public lives, they chose "Frannie" and "Hans."

Before I wrote this book, I had written my childhood reflections on family events. Some of those stories are included here. A few others express family embellishments on stories about my mother.

—F.D.N.

Frances Dean Wilcox Nolde

INTRODUCTION TO
Frances Dean Wilcox Nolde

"Foxy Frannie," my mother, was a beautiful, generous, smart, energetic actress, wife, mother, and pioneer aviator, who became a strong voice for women during World War II and for aviation during the Cold War.

After more than 80 years, I search for the essence of my mother through the lens of my childhood memories, myths, and wide-eyed emotions. Family stories, newspaper articles, and photographs help fill in facts I never knew as the youngest of seven children. As an adult, I want others to know about Mother's life because she influenced the world of aviation when women weren't revered or respected. She gave to her family the values and beliefs she held dear, particularly the importance of education and independence. As I interpret the times, I have come to understand how my mother's challenges influenced my own life.

Frannie set out to become an opera star, entering Oberlin College at the age of 16. The death of her mother shattered her dream. After college, the closest she came to opera stardom was in the chorus of an Adele and Fred Astaire Broadway musical. After a short-lived marriage and divorce, Frannie played the title role in *Gloria Gay's Affairs*, a popular radio soap opera. Her New York adventure ended when Hans Nolde, father of four children, convinced her to marry him and move to his mansion in Pennsylvania with her daughter. Frannie had two more children with Hans.

While raising seven children in a demanding household, she became an accomplished pilot, winner of the All-Women's Transcontinental Air Race, known as the "Powder Puff Derby," and director of the women's program in the Civil Air Patrol. Colonel Frances Dean Wilcox Nolde had reached the highest rank allowed a woman.

Throughout her life, family and friends came to know her many-layered personality. Some marveled only at her beauty. Some thrilled at her ambition and drive. Some respected her talent and intellect. Some felt her loving nature. Some rankled at her demanding, critical tendencies. Others adored her, no matter what she did or believed, regardless of her narcissism and egocentricity.

Complex. Cosmopolitan. Hiding her deepest hurts and emotions, Mother was a complicated woman, an enigma.

This is her story, seen through the eyes of her youngest child, Frances Dean Nolde.

Fountain, Nolde Forest Home

PART ONE

Performer

MAYOR'S REPORT

President Wilcox Submits Report as President of Village.

CHAPTER ONE

Early Years

• DEPOSIT, NEW YORK •

In 1898, Mother's parents, Elizabeth (neé Lewis) and Frederick Wilcox, were married and settled in a small, upstate New York town called Deposit. Four years later, they named their second daughter Frances Dean Wilcox, after her fraternal grandmother, and they called her Frannie.

Early photographs reveal a sweet-looking girl enjoying her family and privileged station in life. She wore large taffeta bows in her hair, gingham dresses, and patent leather Mary Janes. Surrounded by family members of all generations, she looked serene and happy.

Frederick Dean Wilcox was a well-liked, well-off businessman who became Mayor of Deposit. Among his many successes, he was a spirited harness race competitor, horse breeder, and trainer of pacers. His ancestors were the first settlers of Deansville, a village that became part of Deposit. *The Hudson Valley Sojourner* says the name Deposit "was derived from the deposits of logs made by lumbermen, prior to forming rafts to float down the Delaware River."

With her older sister Catherine

Frannie's large bow

Older sister Catherine and their mother, Elizabeth

With Grandpa Lewis

During college years

• OBERLIN AND FATHER •

During her schooling, Frannie had skipped two grades, joining the 1918 high school class of her older sister Catherine. As a girl, Frannie had learned to love opera, probably from her piano or guitar teachers. And perhaps the family listened to live Metropolitan Opera radio broadcasts, which began in 1910. So, at 16, Frannie began a music program at Oberlin College to pursue a career as an opera singer.

Frannie's dream abruptly ended when her mother became ill with breast cancer. Frannie attended Oberlin from September 1, 1918, until January 1, 1919, with no record of academic credits. She repeatedly said her father insisted she leave Oberlin, most likely to care for her mother, who died six months after Frannie returned home. At the age of 17, Frannie lost the opportunity to observe life and talk about it with her mother; she was left to figure out relationships on her own.

The following fall, her father, a no-nonsense man, sent Frannie to Syracuse University, with its focus on liberal arts and where her older sister Catherine could look after her. But in college, Catherine paid little attention to her younger sister. Frannie directed the shock and grief of her mother's death at her father, furious with him for prohibiting her return to Oberlin. She never forgave him and never went back home. Only later did Frannie learn she didn't have a voice for opera.

In 1919, Frannie began as a freshman at Syracuse. For her first three years, she studied in the School of Fine Arts, pursuing a bachelor of music degree. In her senior year, she switched to the Teachers College from which she earned a bachelor of science degree in music (sometimes referred to as a bachelor of science degree in public school music).

Later in life, Frannie expressed anger at her father in indirect ways — her sorrow in disguise. She rarely talked about him with her children, nor did she visit him at his family home in Deposit. She did, however, prop two photographs of him on her dresser: one, a causal portrait; the other, showing him racing as a sulky driver holding the reins behind a high-stepping pacer.

When interviewed about her flying career, Frannie said, "I guess I started flying because my father had a string of race horses, and I wanted to go him one better."

She always remembered her mother, Elizabeth Lewis Wilcox, as a lovely, kind woman. Frannie shared with her own children a watercolor Elizabeth had painted many years before — a soft seascape with a milky blue sky and sand dunes.

Despite her negative emotions toward her father, Frannie demonstrated the importance of family and kept Wilcox family ties through her sisters and other relatives. She also remained close to her own mother's family, the Lewises.

In 1940, she did attend her father's funeral which I well remember because the family left me behind. As the youngest of seven, I remember my brother Chris taunting me, saying I was too little to go. I was three-and-a-half.

HER FATHER'S HORSE

My grandfather Wilcox and his harness race partner, Ray G. Pratt, owned pacers, and Fred Wilcox raced them with great success, particularly the horses known as Prince Abbe, Walter Dale, and Hal Cochato. When Fred Wilcox died, the partnership dissolved, and Hal Cochato went to a stable in Connecticut for a "satisfactory price for Mrs. Wilcox's benefit." Mother never mentioned her father had remarried.

When I was 11, I began English saddle riding lessons at the barn of our family friend, Sam Fry. Mother decided to purchase Hal Cochato for me to ride. I soon found it would take a while to break a harness pacer to the saddle, but eventually Hal Cochato was boarding at

Sam's barn, and I was riding him. I learned that a pacer could outrun any horse's gallop, but Hal Cochato was not accustomed to fording streams or going up or down a hill: He would balk and rear until, finally, he'd agree to do what I asked of him.

At the time, I had no idea what it meant for Mother to bring one of her father's pacers home for me to ride. I now understand her generosity of spirit and Daddy's willingness to spend the money to buy and re-train this splendid horse. I also understand Mother's conflicted relationship with her father: She was angry with him but loved him at the same time.

When Mother turned 90, I hoped she would finally tell me about her father. When I asked, she became angry at me for trying to nudge something out of her. Dead silence. She carried her anger to her deathbed, but she must also have felt great sadness.

Fred Wilcox racing a pacer

• BROADWAY DREAMS •

As she was graduating from Syracuse in 1923, Frannie was thinking of marrying her college sweetheart, G. Carlton Brown, nicknamed Kharki. In April, they applied for a marriage certificate, but they didn't use it. Instead, Frannie moved to Clyde, New York, 50 miles west of Syracuse. What she did there no one seems to know, but she did receive letters in Clyde from Dick, an admirer who wanted to know if he stood a chance or if she still loved Kharki. Mother wrote Dick that she was willing to see him, but she was not encouraging.

As a fine pianist and teacher, and with her Syracuse degree in arts and sciences, Frannie soon left Clyde to become a supervisor of music in the public schools of Orange, New Jersey. But that job was short-lived, as operatic and theatrical dreams called her to Broadway.

Frannie joined the ensemble of *Lady, Be Good,* George and Ira Gershwin's first Broadway hit, starring Fred Astaire and his sister Adele. It's not clear just how long a run Frannie had during the show's 330 performances between 1924 and 1925, but we do know that she next joined the cast of *The Best of Us* which opened in Cincinnati, moved to Detroit, and after a two-week run, closed.

Twenty-five years later, Frannie told *The Philadelphia Inquirer Magazine,* "On the last night in Detroit, the scenery fell down and hit the stage manager. That was the crowning blow. The show folded and so did my career."

"To Frances With Love from Fred"

Adele Astaire, 1920s, in Lady Be Good

• KHARKI AND SALLY •

While Frannie pursed her dreams as a music teacher and then on Broadway, Kharki remained in Syracuse as a reporter for the *Syracuse Post-Standard*. He continued to court Frannie from afar after he became secretary to Syracuse Mayor Charles Hanna. Mayor Hanna's initiative to bring air travel to Syracuse in 1927 would have pleased Frannie years later. As Kharki sharpened his considerable writing skills, he also convinced Frannie to return to Syracuse. They took out a new marriage certificate; this time they did marry, on May 31, 1926, and Frannie became Frances Dean Wilcox Brown.

Frannie's first child, a daughter, was born the following year. They named her Consuelo, most likely after the title character in George Sand's romantic novel, but the name did not stick. They decided to call her Sally.

Although Kharki was a talented writer, his alcoholism soon led Frannie to end the marriage, and she left Syracuse with Sally, heading for work back in New York City.

As Sally grew up, Frannie helped her daughter remain connected to her father. In time, Kharki overcame his alcoholism and became a successful Hollywood script writer. In the mid-1940s, he collaborated in writing the play *School for Brides* which ran on Broadway for almost a year. Television was growing, and beginning with *My Little Margie* in the mid-1950s, G. Carleton Brown created popular comedy scripts for many early TV shows, including *The People's Choice* and *McHale's Navy*.

Mother wanted Sally to know and sustain connections with Kharki's family, flying her to the Thousand Islands each summer to visit the Browns. When Sally was older, she flew to California to visit her father, his second wife Emily, and their daughter Robin. Sally and her half-sister Robin formed a strong bond during those visits.

Mother and Sally

Sally's affection for Robin was complicated by intense competition for their father's attention and approval, just as sibling rivalry became common in the Nolde household. After Emily's death, the half-sisters grew apart; Kharki remarried and moved to Mexico, and Sally seldom communicated with him.

CHAPTER TWO

Gloria Gay

After she divorced Kharki in the late 1920s, Frannie took Sally to New York where she began to work in radio for NBC, portraying glamorous Gloria Gay, the lead in the weekly 15-minute soap opera *Gloria Gay's Affairs*. For the character, Frannie developed a convincing, sophisticated British accent. Later, when she was interviewed on the radio about her flying, that same accent came alive. She was often asked if she were English. Much later, when I was interviewed for work or other activities, people would ask if I were British. I must have unconsciously imitated her.

Gloria Gay promo picture

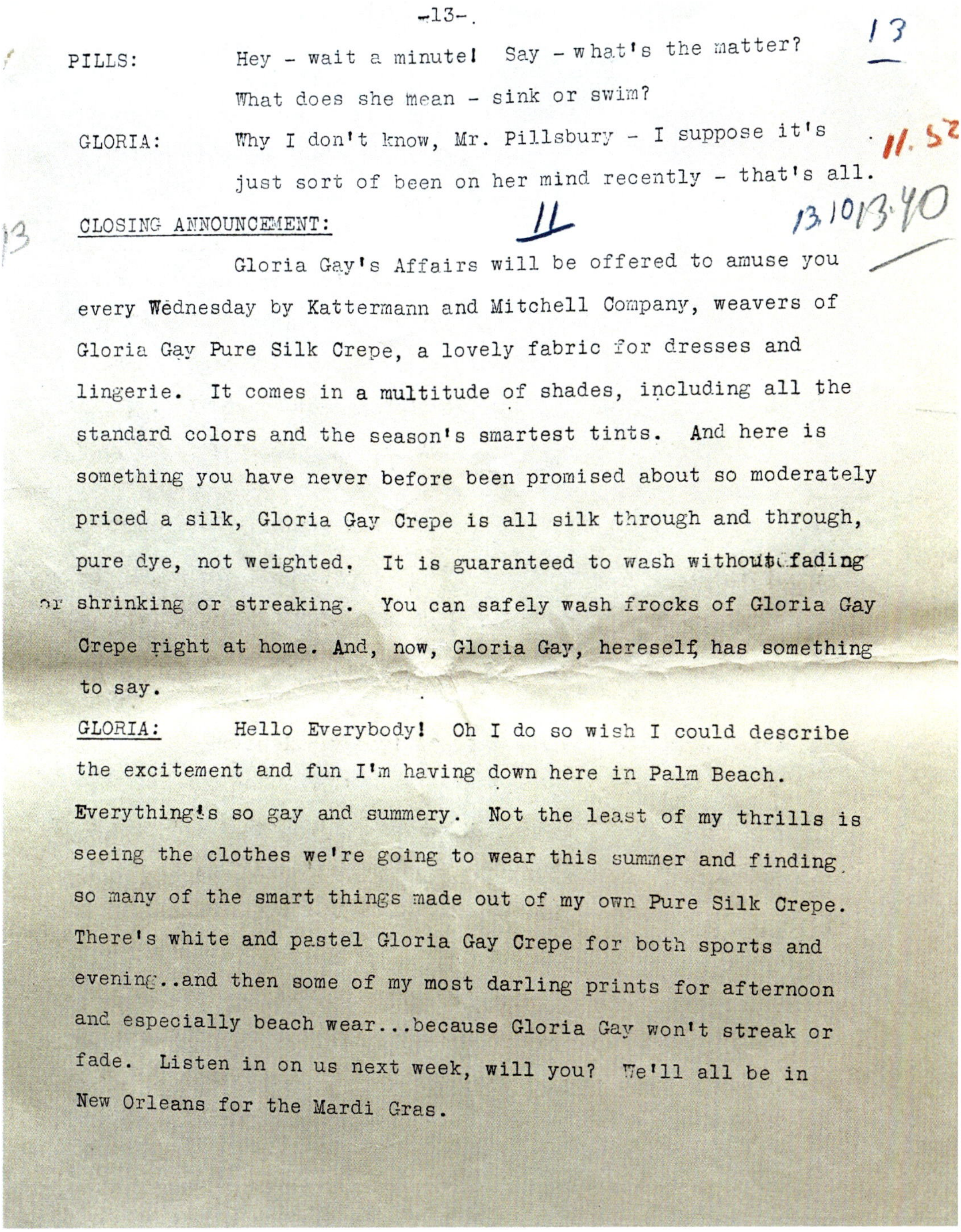

-13-

PILLS: Hey - wait a minute! Say - what's the matter? What does she mean - sink or swim?

GLORIA: Why I don't know, Mr. Pillsbury - I suppose it's just sort of been on her mind recently - that's all.

CLOSING ANNOUNCEMENT:

Gloria Gay's Affairs will be offered to amuse you every Wednesday by Kattermann and Mitchell Company, weavers of Gloria Gay Pure Silk Crepe, a lovely fabric for dresses and lingerie. It comes in a multitude of shades, including all the standard colors and the season's smartest tints. And here is something you have never before been promised about so moderately priced a silk, Gloria Gay Crepe is all silk through and through, pure dye, not weighted. It is guaranteed to wash without fading or shrinking or streaking. You can safely wash frocks of Gloria Gay Crepe right at home. And, now, Gloria Gay, hereself, has something to say.

GLORIA: Hello Everybody! Oh I do so wish I could describe the excitement and fun I'm having down here in Palm Beach. Everything's so gay and summery. Not the least of my thrills is seeing the clothes we're going to wear this summer and finding so many of the smart things made out of my own Pure Silk Crepe. There's white and pastel Gloria Gay Crepe for both sports and evening..and then some of my most darling prints for afternoon and especially beach wear...because Gloria Gay won't streak or fade. Listen in on us next week, will you? We'll all be in New Orleans for the Mardi Gras.

A final page from Gloria Gay's Affairs, *program #20*

February 11, 1931
Modeling for her radio series' sponsor, Gloria Gay's pure silk crepe

By now, Frannie had gained public attention, and the press noticed her resemblance to Marlene Dietrich. It was no surprise that Frannie's friend, George Long, told her she should meet someone who was crazy about her in her role as Gloria Gay: Hans Nolde, a hosiery magnate from Pennsylvania. At first, Frannie was not interested and repeatedly put George off until she no longer could resist his entreaties. Once Hans arrived in New York, he must have swept her off her feet — either that or she was tired of trying to pursue an acting career. Hans' first wife had run off to California with a man ten years her junior, leaving Hans with four young children. A commitment to Hans meant a commitment to not only Sally but four more children. Frannie said, "Yes."

Marlene Dietrich

PART TWO

Parent

Surrounded by three of five children, (l. to r.) Jake, Sally, and Jeanne, the newlyweds enjoy summer.

CHAPTER THREE

Pennsylvania Dutch Beginning

• JOYFUL MERGER •

Frannie and Hans married in 1933, settling in the outskirts of Reading in an area known as Sheerlund where Nolde relatives lived in contiguous estates. Fashioned after an English Tudor castle, Hans' mansion sat on what became 725 acres of German pine forest and woodlands. He ran a household with a staff of eight that included a forester and the forester's helpers whom Hans called "the men." Several newspaper articles claimed the castle had 22 rooms, a slight exaggeration, even if you counted the wine cellar and the "blackout," canning, and laundry rooms.

The estate was called "Punches Run," after the stream that ran through the property, "run" being the Pennsylvania Dutch term for "creek." The source for the name "Punches" remains a mystery. Hans called the property "The Place."

This was Pennsylvania Dutch Country. Amish families living in Angelica, a hamlet "down the road a piece," went to Reading on a small bus that stopped at our driveway to pick up Chris and me when we were old enough to go into the city alone. Captivated, I stared in wonder at the women all looking alike, with black caps over hair tied in a bun and aprons over calico dresses. Little girls wore small copies of their mothers' dresses, and the young boys wore wide-brimmed black hats.

At home, we indulged in Pennsylvania Dutch food, such as scrapple, shoofly pie, Schmoyer's rye bread with apple butter, and thin German pancakes with grape jelly and confectioner's sugar sprinkled over them. Occasionally, instead of table linen, place mats covered our dining room table with quaint Pennsylvania Dutch sayings like, "Throw Papa Down the Stairs His Hat." Or, "Papa's on the Table and Half Et Already."

Hans — Papa — was a hunter and fisherman who took an annual trip to Canada to hunt black bear and deer. He didn't hunt on the family property, but he did stock the stream with trout each spring. The trout rarely stayed in the deep pools Hans had prepared, so when he went fishing, using special liver as bait, the trout would have moved downstream. We teased him for never catching one of his own fish. Ever.

By then, Frannie had lived through the First World War (1914-18), the Spanish Flu (1918-20,) the success of women's suffrage in 1920, the Roaring Twenties, the Crash of 1929, and the beginning of the Great Depression (1929-39). In 1933, when she left a tough, independent, glamorous Manhattan acting career for a new marriage in Pennsylvania, she began a life that afforded her access to wealth, polite society, lavish parties with flowing alcohol, and connection to the Nolde reputation. Nevertheless, she retained her independence.

Daddy playing Charlie Chaplin with an axe

Front of "The Place." Note the weather vane, a witch.

Covered porch with wisteria

Frannie now found herself in a handsome home, full of Hans' vision of a magical place for his large family. While it resembled a small castle, its windows brought in light, sometimes through a charming, poetic story in stained glass. And the doors were modest in size, welcoming for children.

Many details of the house reflected Hans' sense of humor and whimsey. The iron weathervane on the castle's roof was a witch riding a broom. The boot scraper on the outside threshold was an arched black cat, terrified of the witch. The playroom doorknob was a jester blowing a horn. And the brass doorknob leading into the dining room was in the shape of a baker, holding in his left hand a spoon and offering in his right hand a pie that you pushed down to open the latch. Humpty Dumpty opened the outside door to the playroom.

To honor Frannie and Hans' 15th wedding anniversary, their matchmaker, George Long, wrote this corny poem:

"THE COURTSHIP OF FRANCES BY HANS"

How well do I remember
That Spring of '33.
The lovely voice of Gloria Gay
Was heard on N.B.C.

Her voice was pleasing to the ear;
Her face we could not see,
For television was still
An unknown mystery.

A gentleman from Sheerlund,
Whom we all know quite well,
Became enamored of this voice;
In love he deeply fell.

No other program mattered.
His dial he did not twirl.
One thought kept torturing him –
"I gotta meet this girl."

His love overcame his shyness,
For mighty shy was he.
His dilemma he confided
To a friend named Long, that's me.

His friend said, "Your problem's ended.
I know the toast of New York town.
She's even lovelier than her voice;
Her name is Frances Brown."

So George arranged the meeting
For Hans and the beauteous Fran.
She murmured as she met him,
"What a gorgeous hunk of man!"

The attraction it was mutual
And instantaneous too.
No mere casual friendship this,
As they both rightly knew.

They arranged to meet for luncheon
At the Ritz on the morrow;
But Hansel he did not appear
To Frances' great sorrow.

Our hero he was sleeping
At the Hotel Vanderbilt,
Dreaming of himself and Fran,
With never a thought of guilt.

The thrill of finally meeting
His dream lady, you see,
Had completely exhausted our hero;
He finally awoke at three.

Great was his consternation
When he noticed the time.
He bowed his head in sorrow;
He bowed his head in shyme.

He hied real fast to Frances,
And pled upon his knees;
And she, kind soul, was most impressed
With his heartbroken pleas.

She graciously forgave him.
She knew his sterling worth.
They were married in New Jersey
On October the fourth.

In Englewood, New Jersey,
In 1933;
So please arise and drink a toast
To their crystal jublilee.

CHAPTER FOUR

Knitting a Family and a Life

Now part of a knitted family — a rather unique situation for the times — Sally joined the four Nolde children in the care of their mature, loyal, and beloved nanny, "Bysie" Price, who came to the house daily. When Bysie first arrived, the Nolde children's mother Peg had said, "Now pay attention to your Nanny! Bye." That's how Bysie got her name. Bysie often entertained the children by driving them in a pony-drawn cart around the front circle and down the long driveway. Sally was six; Hans' children were Jake six, Jeanne eight, Bobby 12, and Johnny 14.

I can only imagine how difficult those early years were for the five of them. Sally said that at first she was picked on and ignored by the Nolde children until they finally accepted her into the family after she formed a bond with the youngest, Jake.

Hans and Frannie went on to have two more children of their own. Hans Christopher was known as "Hansel" until he became "Chris" when German names raised suspicion during WWII. And then I arrived — Francie. The family jokingly or affectionately called us "Hansel and Gretel," but we were not of major interest to the five other children. Still, we were included in most family rituals and games, especially at Christmastime, or when we were lured to flop down on our stomachs in the large entrance hall to play a fast, slap-dash game of quadruple solitaire — a game we never won.

Being a stepmother to four children, guiding and helping Sally make the adjustment to having four half-siblings, and then bringing two babies into the mix, must have been challenging for Mother. She had to take charge of three sets of children, referee disagreements, and meet the demands of the five older ones while meeting the needs of two little ones. She developed different relationships with each of us, but we never doubted her love. What I heard was her kind and interested tone. Some of the children sought her affection; some were jealous of the affection she gave others; some were more distant, some closer. I was too young to understand the nuances of Mother's multidimensional relationships with us.

Johnny was 18 and off to Cornell when I was born. In 1942, at age five, I was the flower girl for Bobby, my oldest half-sister, at her Punches Run wedding. At six, I became an aunt to her baby boy. From my perspective, the older Noldes were out of reach, although Jeannie was affectionate toward Chris and me. We adored her in return, especially because she drove us around in Daddy's yellow Jeep. Sally, ten years older, invited me sit on her bed to have long conversations when she was a teenager. I loved her, too.

When I was very young, Daddy called me "Sunshine," as if it were my only name. At the end of every Sunday breakfast, he'd save some of his freshly squeezed orange juice in the bottom of his glass and invite me to sit on his lap, saying "Come on over, Sunshine, I have something for you." Then he would hand me his glass with about an inch of juice in it. I drank in his love at the same time I drank the juice. I always waited to see if he would remember the juice — and he did.

When I was about eight, I was also nourished by my early morning walks in the woods. I would wake up before anyone else, get dressed, and tiptoe out of the castle to walk along the dirt road that led me deep into the forest. Many years later, I realized I had discovered something I couldn't put into words at the time. I felt safe and protected by Nature and the Universe.

Mother and Daddy had no formal religion. They left me to develop my own path, which led me to love our Punches Run forest with its

animals and creatures, sounds and smells, all unique to the woods. As an adult, I still call myself a "wood nymph." Until I was eleven, I tried to spend every summer morning in the woods for about an hour. I'd then return home for my own glass of freshly squeezed orange juice.

In one of Daddy's letters to Jeanne, he wrote, "Francie, of course, is as good as gold as usual, and very seldom complains about anything she has to do, but she is turning into some kind of actress because she can't even talk without acting in some form or another." His description was apt.

• EXTRAVAGANT SOCIAL LIFE •

Hans and Frannie entertained regularly by holding large cocktail parties for their country club friends and those considered part of the Reading social scene. Glimmering candelabra and platters, crystal, and silverware shone brightly to welcome the guests. While Chris and I passed hors d'oeuvres, alcohol flowed generously in our smoke-filled living room. The kitchen staff worked relentlessly to keep ahead of the demand for food and drink. After we went to bed, laughter echoed long into the night.

On Thursdays and Sundays, "cook's night out," our family went to dinner at a private club, dressed in our best clothes. Despite being bored by the adult conversation, my brother and I were taught to behave politely.

• LOVE OF OPERA •

Mother brought to Punches Run her teenage passion for opera. On Saturdays she asked the family to join her in the library to listen to Texaco's Metropolitan Opera radio matinees hosted by Milton Cross. I sat through many performances, squirming until I was finally allowed to leave. Years later, in the mid-1950s, Mother took me to dinner at a Washington restaurant where operatic singers performed arias. As she listened intently to the dramatic, melodious voices, Mother became teary, most likely thinking of her dashed dreams of becoming an opera star.

• MAGICAL CHRISTMAS •

Relying upon her theatricality, Mother created a fairy-tale Christmas, particularly for the younger children. About ten days before Christmas, Daddy would go into the woods with Johnny or Jake, and sometimes one of the men, and cut from the German forest just the right Christmas tree. The 15-foot tree presented a challenge as it was hauled to the house and placed in the open spiral staircase in the tower, with the tree's tip tucked into the bottom of the chandelier. Quickly the house filled with the scent of the Tannenbaum.

After dinner on Christmas Eve, we'd go into the living room to stand around the grand piano and sing carols. I wondered why Christmas Eve was the only time Mother played; when asked, she never explained. Sometimes Mother invited Sally to play or Jake (who could play but one carol). It was a loving, exciting family time. After singing, we ran to our rooms to gather stockings to hang on the mantel. Daddy helped me hang mine, the tiniest, at one end. The first year I hung my stocking, I felt shocked by the small size in comparison to everyone else's, but by morning, all the stockings were magically transformed into the same size.

The tree remained in its natural state until the end of Christmas Eve, when the younger children were packed off to bed while our parents and older siblings decorated the tree with lights and colorful, delicate, European Christmas tree bulbs. When we woke up in the morning, we rushed to the staircase to melt into the magic of a tree completely transformed.

The thrill of Christmas morning became even more intense when we were not allowed to enter the living room until we finished breakfast: freshly squeezed orange juice, scrambled eggs, and different kinds of stollen, a German sweet bread sent by relatives — all too much for my over-stimulated stomach.

After a long wait, we lined up in the hall, the youngest first and Daddy last, to march into the living room to find a roaring fire and chairs filled to the brim with presents for each family member. As the youngest, I opened my presents first, a mixed blessing because I had to wait until everyone's presents were opened before I could play with my new toys and dolls.

Mother's generosity and kindness shone when she invited "Nana," the older Nolde children's maternal grandmother, to join us for Christmas dinner. Daddy would drive into Reading, pick Nana up, and bring her to Punches Run for the rest of the day. She looked somber in her long, black dress. She entertained Chris and me by reading the same book every year, *Pauline, the Little Match Girl.* Then she'd lecture us about never, ever striking matches. Her admonition made us very curious because Daddy had already taught us how to strike a match properly and would let us light his cigarettes and pipe.

When Nana died, Mother asked me if I'd like to go into town to the wake. Not knowing what a wake was, I nodded, "Yes." When the evening arrived and we entered the building, I could see a coffin at the end of the dimly lit room, with people walking up to it. Mother asked if I wanted to see Nana in the coffin. I declined and waited in the back of the room, scared and relieved.

• BELOVED "CORNBAKE" •

In spring, a short walk through the woods "down back" led to rows of daffodils bordering large open fields. In late May, the men planted hills of Golden Bantam Sweet Corn to ripen in August. By July, we picked wild strawberries to help Mary, the cook, add them to cream and sugar in her old-fashioned, hand-churning ice cream maker. When Chris came home with an empty bucket, we accused him of eating his strawberries. Years later, he learned he was color blind and couldn't distinguish green leaves from red fruit. All summer, we waited for the corn tassels to turn brown.

The main event of every summer was our cornbake for country club friends, Reading Airport colleagues, Civil Air Patrol cadets, extended family, and soldiers, pilots, and Marines home on leave.

Early in the morning, the men would help Daddy select perfect ears of corn, soak them unhusked in buckets of water all day, and gather mounds of wood for an evening fire in the huge, outdoor fireplace. When the logs became chunks of smoldering coal, Daddy and his helpers placed the tinfoil-wrapped corn on top of the grill to steam. Next, they buried the ears in the coals until the corn was fully cooked. Once the husks and kernels were nicely charred, Daddy's grilled chicken and steak, and the smoky smell of corn, invited everyone to the summertime feast.

While many enjoyed the evening at the house, other guests gathered down back to breathe in the smoke, listen to the crackle of the fire, and delight in the nighttime fluttering of moths.

At one wartime cornbake, Mother invited a distant cousin just before he went overseas. The young Marine looked startlingly handsome in his deep blue and red-trimmed uniform with its row of brass buttons down his front, three brass buttons on each of his cuffs, and a single brass button on each pocket and shoulder. He also looked nervous as he quietly told us about his plans. Nine months later, we learned that he had been killed.

• AIR RAID WARNING •

Early in the war, we gathered at Punches Run with a few other families to enjoy a summer's evening. One of Sally's closest friends made a point of spending time with me before bedtime, a highlight of the evening. She said, "Goodnight" as I snuggled into bed with a book.

A few hours later, everyone was shocked to hear the whine of an air raid siren. They turned off all the lights and crept down to the "Blackout Room," where dark shades and heavy curtains blocked out any light while they waited for the blast of the "All-Clear."

Instead, they heard the roar of a fire engine and boots of firemen as they entered the house with large flashlights. One of the firemen rushed upstairs to my room and found me sound asleep with my bedside light on. Gently, without waking me, he turned off the light and rejoined his crew.

The Fire Warden had seen the flicker of my reading light from the road far below and believed the house was on fire. In the depths of a dark forest, mine was the only light the warden saw.

In the morning, I was shocked when they told me about the mishap, but the story made everyone else laugh. I wasn't punished.

• THE ONLY MOTHER •

When Peg, Daddy's first wife, left him and their four children to remarry in California, she seemed to lose interest in her children. I don't remember her sending them birthday or Christmas presents or even cards. Mother was the only mother all seven of us called "Mother."

As a testament to Mother's ability to create equality among the children, I never thought of any of my five half-brothers and sisters as anything but full siblings. I didn't know about half-sisters and half-brothers until I was in high school. Nor did I become aware of differences among human beings based on their skin color or religious beliefs until high school. Despite coming from a white, privileged background, Mother didn't teach us to be prejudiced. Only later did I learn to recognize how my white privilege created injustices for others.

Bobby's wedding to Whit Russell in 1942. Sally is shown in the insert. Top row: Jake, Bobby, Daddy, Johnny. Bottom row: Chris, Francie, Mother, Jeanne.

• JOY WITH MOTHER AND DADDY •

The solid grounding of love I received in my very early years has nurtured me throughout my life. As an adult, I understand, at the most fundamental level, that love endures and needs to be given freely and unconditionally.

While Daddy continued to call me "Sunshine," the rest of the family called me "Tunie." Their friend George Long had looked at me as a newborn and said, "She's as pink as a Petunia!" At first, I was known as "Petunia," then "Tunie."

When I sat next to Mother as she drove, she would affectionately pat my knee and smile down at me. She'd say, "I love you, Tunie." I glowed with happiness. And each night when she tucked me into bed, she sang one of two lullabies: "Lullaby and Goodnight" or two verses of an unusual choice, "My Old Kentucky Home." I loved the melancholy words, "Weep no more, my lady/ Oh, weep no more today/ For we'll sing one song / For my old Kentucky home/ For my old Kentucky home/ Far away." I wouldn't let her stop. I always asked for an encore, and she would oblige. Then she'd caress my arms with her soft touch, giving me goosebumps.

Daddy's bedtime contribution was to read me books. I had a few favorites I asked him to read over and over again. *Gabriel Churchkitten* made me laugh out loud. One Sunday, on a family walk in the woods, I twisted my ankle and fell. Daddy carried me home in his arms. I loved that! Daddy wrapped my sprained ankle in ice and laid me down on my bed. When bedtime rolled around, he started reading about Gabriel, of course. Soon I was laughing, then crying out because my ankle hurt when I laughed. We'd laugh again because I was laughing and then crying with pain, and so it went: hurt and joy together. What a conundrum for a little girl! It was a life lesson, reflected in the many challenges of living in that complex, puzzling family.

Petunia

CHAPTER FIVE

Children On Their Own

By the time I was born, Mother was well on her way to discovering her many talents and interests. Her keen mind would eventually lead her to national recognition. I ask myself now, "What did she give up to become famous as she pursued her newfound interest in flying and wartime endeavors? Anything?"

"Hansel and Gretel"

• FLYING IN THE FAMILY •

Before his marriage to Mother, Daddy had shown interest in flying. In 1927, he and several businessmen founded Reading's airport, coining "Whander Field" from the initials of the founders' last names. Managed by Reading Airways, it became Pennsylvania's first airfield for commercial flying.

Hans began flying lessons himself. His interest in aviation took an adventurous turn when, in 1928, he flew to Germany on the dirigible (gas-filled) *Graf Zeppelin*. After takeoff, he called Peg, his first wife, to say that everything was going smoothly aboard the rigid airship. Hans came home on the new USS *Isle de France*, to be met in New York by Peg, his sister Carol, and Charlie Guthrie, Carol's husband. Family members think he spent about $3,000 for his one-way dirigible ticket, the equivalent of almost $50,000 today. The *Graf Zeppelin* was taken out of service after the 1937 *Hindenburg* disaster, an airship explosion killing 35 people. The brief, rigid-airship era then came to an end.

When Frannie moved to Reading, she became intrigued with flying, too. Daddy must have convinced her to try her hand. She never set out to be a female pioneer in aviation, most likely thinking it a lark to join her new husband in taking flying lessons. However, she fell in love with the exhilaration of being airborne, alone — a true getaway. She admitted to an addiction she never expected! The addiction brought consequences. Sometimes, my brother and I ran wild when left alone in the castle.

To have time to fly, Mother hired a succession of nannies to help with caring for Chris and me. Chris and I would have none of it. We wanted our mother's care and attention, so we lied to each nanny, made it impossible for her to care for us, ran away and hid, and told her we hated her. We were insufferable! We succeeded in getting three nannies to quit. We hoped each would be the last, but Mother kept replacing them. Finally, Mother gave up, so during the summer, she left us home alone with other household help. That was a mistake; we became even bigger troublemakers. Acting up became second nature to Chris and me.

Left alone in the big house, with nothing to do but plot and rig adventures, we roamed around, sometimes searching for loose change in Daddy's jacket pockets, on bureau tops, under couch pillows, or in chests of drawers. When we were confident none of the help were around, we would short sheet their beds, drink beer under the guest room bed, and best of all, drive the Jeep all over the property.

On one such day, we went into Mother's walk-in closet, where we opened and closed cupboards only to discover a Smith and Wesson revolver lying in a drawer filled with silk scarves. We handed it back and forth as we talked about how scary it was to hold, and then we returned it to its hiding place. What if we had pointed it at each other and said, "Bang, bang, you're dead," or pulled the trigger? Was it loaded? We didn't know. A week later, we came back for another look. It was gone!

• THREE ESCAPADES OF MANY •

In the autobiographical stories I later wrote about growing up at Punches Run, I describe three of our escapades involving beer, cigarettes, and the yellow Jeep.

Good Old Reading Beer

When Chris was ten and I was eight, we decided to act grown up by drinking beer. We knew where a stash of Old Reading Beer stood waiting in the huge built-in refrigerator. Our brother Jake had bought several cases for a party.

On the afternoon of the party, Chris and I carefully pried open a number of beer bottles and poured some of the beer down the drain.

Giggling, we filled the bottles with water and carefully replaced the caps. Thrilled to trick unsuspecting drinkers, we awaited the evening's festivities. That night, we snuck down to the kitchen and stole four unopened beer bottles. We rushed up the back stairs.

Two glasses and a beer opener lay waiting under the guest room bed, our hideout. We slithered in. Chris opened two bottles, and we began to drink. I tried valiantly but didn't like the taste.

While Chris finished his beer, I became fearful of discovery. We snuck back downstairs to return the unopened bottles. I shook, worried that someone would stumble upon us. Relieved not to be caught, we tiptoed back to bed.

No one ever mentioned weak or watery beer. Disappointed, we never fiddled with the beer again. Weren't the adults clever to handle us that way? Or didn't they notice?

Big-time Smokers

For a period of time, after Mother tucked us in bed and said, "Goodnight," Chris and I smoked in bed. We hid everything we needed in our bedside tables: cigarettes, cigarette holders with filters (like Daddy's), cigars, old pipes with chewed off ends, tobacco, pipe cleaners, matches, and an ashtray.

When positioned correctly, the long mirror on the inside of my closet door gave me a view of the hall from my bed, all the way down to my parents' bedroom. After we went to bed, this built-in lookout system alerted us to anyone walking up the hall.

Five minutes after being tucked in, I'd whisper to Chris, "Coast's clear." We'd run into our separate bathrooms, fill up glasses with water, and put them by our beds.

Pulling a long Pall Mall from the pack, I squeezed my little lips around it. As it uncontrollably bobbed up and down, I opened the match cover, tugged off a match, struck it several times, and lit up. The routine went this way: Take in a puff, close the lips tight, hold it, then blow the smoke out fast with a swishing sound, and reach for a gulp of water.

I performed this maneuver over and over again until the cigarette was half the size, and I couldn't take any more. Enjoy it? Can't say I did. But the thrill of repeatedly doing something naughty, and of imitating my parents, made the moment irresistible.

Before long, Mother searched my bedside drawer when I wasn't home. I was shocked to learn of her raid, feeling angry about her sneaky invasion of my room. She was shocked, too, for different reasons.

Earlier, I had indirectly alluded to my clandestine activities. I wanted to get caught in order to end the habit of most nights. Appalled and worried, Mother followed her hunch and scooped everything away from both of us. I tried to recover my stash but contended with a vigilant mother who kept all supplies under wraps.

We weren't punished like others before us, however — only humiliated by the indirect confrontation. When caught smoking, our older siblings had to sit outside in the vestibule and smoke a whole pack. All but one of my five half-siblings became addicted and died from cigarettes or alcohol, or both.

Jim and his wife were "the couple" who lived in the back quarters. They cleaned the house and did odd jobs. I wrote a description of Jim's involvement with us:

The Yellow Jeep

After World War II, Daddy bought a surplus Army Jeep and painted it bright yellow. Like a family mascot, the Jeep played a major role in our lives. Our sister Jeanne drove us around to explore the property. Top off, windshield down.

When he was ten, Chris pleaded with Jim to teach him to drive the Jeep. After much hesitation and outright refusal, Jim gave in. The lessons began. When I objected to being left out, they both tried to teach me, but I couldn't get the hang of shifting. A frustrated and disappointed eight-year-old, I let Chris drive for the two of us.

Knowing the keys were left in the ignition, Chris would invite me to go for a ride. Off we'd go. Top off, windshield down. Smiling and giggling. We drove only on the property and never encountered anyone on the narrow, single-lane roads.

One day, we hopped into the Jeep for another daredevil drive. Loving the bumps, Chris liked to go fast. Begging him to slow down, I'd hold on for dear life. But he'd only laugh and go faster and do daring things, like quickly swerving to the right, then to the left.

After a while, we headed down an unexplored offshoot. Not knowing the road, Chris tempered his speed, so I was having a delightful time. All of a sudden, we came to the end of the road. In front of us loomed the highway.

Our narrow road with deep gullies on either side meant that turning around would likely leave us stuck in the mud or toppled over. But going on the main road could mean detection. We faced a dilemma. Either choice meant discovery, punishment, and humiliation — an end to our carefree joy rides.

Praying we'd meet no oncoming cars, we opted to make a dash for it on the main road. After a car went by, Chris revved up and swung out to the left.

Although Chris drove very fast, for me time shifted into slow motion. We passed familiar sights I could barely see because my arms and hands covered my bent head and lowered eyes. My heart was racing, and I was shaking inside. After a few more agonizing minutes, we neared the entrance to Punches Run. We needed only a second or two more to make it unseen. Would we get there in time? Yes, we would. We Did! Top off, windshield down.

On one summer's day, we discovered that instead of leaving the keys in the ignition, our parents had hidden them. Crestfallen, clever Chris took a day to figure out where they were hidden. Less frequently, we continued our joy rides, but we were sure to return the keys to their hiding place.

• SUBTLE PARENTING •

As the two youngest children, we were rarely punished for our misdeeds. Our parents' strategy was to try to make it impossible for us to continue our antics. Their usual way to deal with our transgressions — be it drinking beer, playing with a revolver, smoking in bed, or driving the Jeep — was to hide or remove the dangerous objects without reasoning with us or explaining. We were expected to figure out that they disapproved and then change our wayward ways. Occasionally, we'd be sent to our rooms for speaking or behaving badly. I remember Mother sending me to my room for yelling, "I hate you!" We knew right from wrong but had no desire to stop what we were doing; we were bored and wanted to amuse ourselves.

But our mischief revealed more than just amusement. We grew up in a home unlike many, though we thought it was what every kid experienced. We were spoiled, had everything we wanted ... AND we were neglected while our parents went about their business. Our mischief became an unanswered call for guidance and parental care.

As an adult, I found it difficult to teach myself how to parent. When raising my two daughters, I didn't have a model for teaching common sense, morality, sexuality, ethics, values, or compassion. I found snippets of advice here and there. Perhaps that's all anyone ever gets. As a mother, I had to rely on reason and intuition to guide me. As I mulled things over, I was slow to act.

I wanted to raise Laurel and Lexi to feel loved and have them know they were worthy of love. I tried to make them feel secure and safe, to teach them ways to become contributors to society, and to find and express joy. I turned to parenting in ways quite different from what I had experienced, but I was not a zealous disciplinarian. I was a liberal parent who hoped my daughters would value themselves, wish to make others' lives better, and find their own happiness. Somehow, I put to good use those early, puzzling years with Mother and Daddy.

• BROTHER CHRIS •

Chris had developed creative ways to garner our parents' attention, perhaps hoping he could distract them from me, the sweet new child. Early home movies show him taking handfuls of dirt and placing them on the wheels of my baby carriage, looking as if he really wanted to throw dirt all over me.

Our easy-going life then changed. Chris contracted scarlet fever and was quarantined for weeks. A special nurse came to the house, and his room was closed to all family members. I missed my playmate. And I was frightened — we all were — as I barely understood what it meant to die but knowing he might not survive. When he finally recovered, all his belongings from that sick room — including toys, books, clothing, and bed linens — were burned in our incinerator.

During middle school, Chris contracted polio and left to live in an iron lung for months at the Sister Kenny Hospital in Philadelphia. Rarely did I hear about his condition, but I knew it was frightening. Once again, Mother worried about his survival.

Polio painfully weakened and disfigured his leg and foot, although an operation helped him regain strength. When he returned to school, nothing stopped him from pitching a rousing no-hitter, and he continued to have a notable high school career in baseball and other sports.

When Chris entered the military, he wanted to be a pilot like Mother, but when he learned he was color blind and didn't qualify, he joined the Army to become a paratrooper. When he left the Army, Chris finished college, studied law at the University of Pennsylvania, and became a successful, highly respected attorney in D.C.

• CONFLICTING KINDNESSES •

Mother was thoughtful and generous; she tried to sense when someone needed extra support. She would step in to help family and friends who were having a tough time. Not until she was much older did she show prejudice for religion or race. Still, she could leave raw wounds by cutting people down fast with criticism if they didn't live up to her standards of excellence.

Mother couldn't always control Chris and me and frequently didn't witness our bad behavior. When I went through a pudgy stage, Chris delighted in pointing at fat people on the street, telling me that was what I would look like soon. Chris and I had little compassion for others, mocking one of the forester's men, saying he was either drunk or slow-witted. We seemed to mimic Mother's critical nature. We had much to unlearn.

Being the youngest, I only understood parts of the discussions I overheard. And no one welcomed my questions. I spent much of my time in the kitchen, talking with the help in their small dining room or "in the back," hanging out in their rooms, listening to the radio, reading comics, or playing games. They were like extended family. Mother made no issue of family status concerning the staff. Only later did she teach me a sense of superiority, a fault I had to overcome in my early 30s when I developed my own set of principles and found my own voice.

Years after Mother's best friend, Dorothy Miller, drowned in a boating accident, Mother brought Dorothy's mom to live with us for a few years. "Auntie Miller" used Sally's old room at the end of the hall, next to Mother and Daddy's bedroom. I loved having her with us. Since I had never known my grandparents, I told Auntie Miller she was now my grandmother. After she left for nursing care, we didn't see her until Mother brought her to live in a nursing home close by until she died. Among a photo collection of special people Mother kept on her dresser sat Auntie Miller's Dorothy.

CHAPTER SIX

Schooling

• "THE NEW SCHOOL" •

Mother wanted her children to have the best possible education. She had a dismal view of the Reading public school system. So before the war, she started a non-profit, private day school called "The New School," offering pre-school and kindergarten through eighth grade. In her six-page description of the purpose and philosophy of the school, she said it would fill a "long-felt need in the community."

Mother was both founder and director. Her advisor was Dr. Margaret Wells who held a Ph.D. from Teachers College, Columbia University. Renowned in her field, Dr. Wells had written several books about education and curriculum, including *A Project Curriculum: Dealing with the Project as a Means of Organizing the Curriculum of the Elementary School*. Mother hired Dr. Ethel James, an associate of Dr. Wells, as head of school. Together, these two women educators selected a staff and put the school in motion. They designed an unusual program for the times, emphasizing a shared central project for each grade, incorporating an interdisciplinary approach that encouraged students to discover ways to integrate mathematics, writing, research, history, and geography into their studies. In addition to an inviting and demanding curriculum, the New School regarded art, music, athletics, and nourishing meals as important to the well-being of young children.

The school attracted 60 students, some of whom were Mother's younger children. I was too young at first but eventually went to kindergarten and first grade there. It opened in the city, in the shadows of Mount Penn, and soon moved out to the country near where we lived, five miles from the center of Reading.

With the bombing of Pearl Harbor, circumstances quickly changed. Stunned, America shifted her role of neutrality to immediate engagement. World War II changed everyday life; rationing of gasoline and supplies eventually forced the school to close its doors.

• BOARDING SCHOOLS •

I felt loved by both my parents until I was sent away to boarding school at the age of six. That event changed everything.

To begin second grade, I had to travel with Chris, Jake, and Jeanne to the Sunny Hills School in Delaware. My older siblings were supposed to take care of me, but I rarely saw them. I ached for Mother and Daddy.

As punishment for my talking during rest hour, teachers either put tape across my mouth or spanked me with a hair brush. When we wrote our weekly letter home, I wanted to say, "Please come get me and take me home. I hate it here." I didn't have the courage. But after Christmas, when everyone was in the car, their luggage in the trunk, ready to return to Sunny Hills, I locked myself in the lavatory. I cried and cried, explaining through the door and through my tears how badly I'd been treated. Finally, Mother relented and convinced me it was safe to come out, telling me I wouldn't have to return. I thought I wouldn't have to go to any school but soon learned I was headed to a local public school to finish second grade.

The next year, Chris and I were sent to the Edgewood School in Greenwich, Connecticut, forcing Chris to leave Sunny Hills, the school he adored. He had no choice. Mother and Daddy told him to accompany me on the train ride and then protect me in the new school, unreasonable demands to make of a nine-year-old boy. I learned much later that this rupture in his life explained his childhood anger at me. I would have been angry, too. As kids, we didn't have the skills to work through emotional issues, and apparently our parents remained oblivious to his feelings, as did I.

Our parents had to handle tuitions, schedules, and travel to boarding schools and colleges for all seven of us. Despite such challenges, once we all were sent away in the fall, Mother and Daddy didn't seem to worry about us till summertime.

• A SIX-YEAR-OLD CHILD •

Far from home at only six, I found news about the war feeding my fears. Well do I remember being terrified and unable to go to sleep for fear of bombs falling on us. I had no understanding about war or the nation's involvement. Were Mother and Daddy expecting me to toughen up? I don't imagine anyone thought about that part of my development. But it didn't work that way. Later in life, my youthful fear of war made me compassionate toward those who suffer from fear and anxiety and led me to work in hospice, family counselling, and grief therapy.

During a visit with Mother when my older daughter had just turned six, I confronted Mother. How could she have sent me away — her youngest — at the age of six? Didn't she know how painful it was for me to be separated from her and Daddy? She immediately said World War II justified her actions. But her rationalization didn't ring true for me because I knew that every day she had made the long drive out to the airport and back. She lived her dream — to fly every day. The sting of this conversation touched me deeply but seemed not to affect her. She never understood how awful the boarding school experience was for me. Living far away from home at such a young age, I felt homesick and frightened by the war. Perhaps she simply had to send us away in order to protect herself from the overwhelming demands of seven children while she committed herself to her wartime responsibilities.

When I was in my 40s, my study of Psychosynthesis covered the topic of family abuse. My colleagues categorically stated that being sent away to boarding school as a young child constituted abuse. They suggested I consider a different perspective on boarding school for young children. Their words shocked me because in wartime, everyone in my family was sent away. Wasn't it normal?

CHAPTER SEVEN

Good Taste

• TO THE MANOR BORN •

Mother had grown up in a beautiful Greek Revival home that graced the rural neighborhood with four oversized, two-story columns. Inside, windows started at the floor and reached to the ceiling. Pictures show her wearing a signature large bow in her hair and a pretty dress as she poses on a horse. Her father could afford to race his pacers and buy new-fangled cars. She had everything a young girl could want. As a child, wealth and advantage were Mother's steady companions, and as an adult, she knew how to bestow the same upon us.

Mother's childhood home

"Dressed" for riding

Riding with younger sister Marjorie and their father

Ever vigilant, Mother demanded proper manners of us. Our behavior reflected upon her, and that mattered. She wanted others to see her as a "good" mother; our appearances and politeness showed that we lacked for nothing. She had been brought up properly and insisted we follow her example:

> Stand up straight ... Sit up straight ... Don't sit with your mouth open ... Don't point your finger at anyone ... Don't make fun of less fortunate people ... Stand up when adults come into the room ... Don't interrupt ... Don't talk with your mouth full ... Chew with your mouth closed ... Stand up straight!!!

We broke her rules at our peril. Following Mother's own pattern, Jeanne left home right after college. Thirty years later, Jeanne told me that Mother had been so critical of her, she fled. I hadn't witnessed Mother and Jeanne's interactions. But as a girl, I watched Mother tear Sally down. I tagged along when Mother took her to the hairdresser and then to a clothing shop, forcing a rebellious daughter into conformity. Mother often diminished us, making me wonder if she had treated Daddy the same way in private.

Mother and her ubiquitous fox stole

Mother trained us to be civil beings who would reflect her exquisite taste. Her trappings included a fox stole and a mink wrap; ermine, beaver, and mink coats; white Irish lace blouses and black velvet skirts; gleaming silver candelabra; silver tea services, bowls, plates, and daily silverware; Meissen china, Scottish hand-sewn table linen, and Jonas Lei paintings. The time and money she spent on selecting beautiful clothes revealed her thirst for attention, respect, and adulation. She was indeed glamorous and accustomed to having all eyes upon her. When she wrangled with Daddy to buy her a new mink coat, Daddy tried to resist Mother's

Appearance has meaning

pleas but couldn't. She wore that coat as a status symbol for years and kept it hanging in her closet long after she was able to hobnob socially. Remembering her past, she found comfort in it. As Mother aged, she used material goods to convey a message: She was above other people and unavailable emotionally.

Mother believed impeccable dressing and grooming completed and preserved a woman's status. She turned heads wherever she went. In the '40s and early '50s, she spent a portion of her morning getting dressed and putting on makeup for the day. She would spend an hour at her dressing table in her spacious bathroom attached to her walk-in closet that contained racks of clothes and a hundred hats. Filled with silk scarves, cashmere sweaters, and lingerie that held the aroma of her perfume, the built-in drawers of all shapes and sizes hid the revolver Chris and I had discovered. Lined up on shoe racks, her assortment of colorful high heels stood ready for any occasion.

Her admiring daughter Sally was the only one allowed to watch and talk with Mother during her morning ritual. Her younger children — Chris and I — had to sit outside on her canopied bed, waiting forever until she came out, beautifully dressed and ready to head to the airport, high heels and all.

• MARRYING "WELL" •

Since appearances meant everything to Mother, she wanted me to impress my fiancé's family. Expecting clothes to say I was worthy of their son and that I came from a privileged background, Mother inappropriately dressed me in black cashmere and her billowing, long, black taffeta evening gown. Her clothes on my back were a misfit for a 20-year-old. I felt ridiculous, but I allowed her to push me to "dress well" and to "marry well." And I did.

During college, my prospects for a job as an English major were dim. I was terrified I would have nowhere to go but to live with

Mother after graduation. The mores of the times encouraged me to "get a ring" by my senior year. Shortly before graduation, two young women in my class broke their engagements. I admired their independence. Even if I wanted to, I didn't have their courage to buck the tide. Instead, I heeded Mother's wishes to find a suitable family to marry into.

When I was engaged, however, I had no one to talk to about marriage — what it is, what it means, or what it brings. In the 1950s, people didn't discuss such things. It would have been wonderful if my parents or older siblings had been capable of discussing issues I didn't understand until much later:

> That a married woman in the '50s might grow in confidence instead of stifling herself by deferring to a husband and society's expectations.
>
> That a wife and husband can support one another as good listeners and partners.
>
> That a wife and husband can learn how to adapt to change, as the relationship and each person develops and grows.

These important possibilities hadn't entered my mind. Not understanding who I was or whom I was marrying, I made a choice based on superficial assumptions. I was 21. Although we looked great in a photograph, shared social connections, and went to the right schools, my husband and I were not well matched. We easily created the "right" appearances, but in the process, I became an empty shell. I had nothing left inside; I broke away in order to survive and breathe once more.

After I divorced my first husband, Mother told me I had no status as a single woman. I had to marry again. Given all Mother had accomplished, she still spoke of the "game" in which women need to be attached to a reputable man's name for recognition. She insisted I play her "game" with one of Chris' friends, a Princeton graduate who matched her idea of a perfect husband. She liked the status of Princeton; she had never met the man nor knew anything about his character. Her advice infuriated me. I was not going to marry for superficial reasons again! I had already married once for the wrong reasons, mostly to gain her approval by marrying for a name, wealth, and all the elements that did not lead to happiness. I wouldn't do that again, and I didn't.

PART THREE

Wife

Daddy and Mother at Johnny's wedding

CHAPTER EIGHT

Marriage

• A DECADE WITH HANS •

When Daddy's eldest son Johnny married Nancy Kurtz during WWII, my parents went to California to witness the joyful ceremony. Johnny stood tall in his Army uniform. My parents looked relaxed and happy.

Johnny and Nancy's marriage certificate has Mother's and Daddy's signatures but also those of Johnny's mother, Peg, and her husband, Savage Klein. Only in discovering the marriage certificate did I learn of Johnny having any connection to his mother in California. "G.G." follows Daddy's signature, the initials of the nickname Johnny gave him, "Grumpy Gramp." Daddy seemed far from grumpy to me.

WWII wedding party (l. to r.) Savage, Johnny, Peg, Nancy, Hans, Frannie

Snyder

• CHANGES •

In the years that followed, however, something put a rent in our parents' relationship. Johnny characterized the disparity between them by not only calling Daddy "Grumpy Gramp" but also calling Mother "Foxy Frannie." Those nicknames seemed to foreshadow the growing break.

At the war's end, Daddy struggled to be kind and civil, but he was out of sorts because business wasn't progressing. And Mother was having the time of her life, becoming independent and self-sufficient as she gained national recognition as a pilot.

Secret lovers may have messed with their relationship. I remember a U.S. Senator coming to visit her. They had some kind of special bond, but Mother didn't seem inclined to pursue it. When I was going through my own divorce, Mother commented that I would have many loves in my lifetime. I didn't want to hear that.

One day when I was about eight, I looked for games in the playroom cupboard and found a small stash of love letters addressed to Mother. Years later, I wrote a fictionalized, dramatized version of what I remember:

Loves Lost

Sitting on the floor of our playroom, I held ten handwritten letters. A newspaper scrap sat in my lap. At my feet curled a long peach-colored satin ribbon that had tied the letters into a tiny bundle. An innocent-looking shoebox lay on its side. Two of the letters told the story of a reignited relationship over a period of eight months, starting in April and ending in January.

April 12, 1947

My Dear,

I was delighted to see you this past week, after so many years. I've been trying to remember — in New York, I think, when you had your radio show. Perhaps as many as 16 years?

You are as beautiful as ever.

Please call me when you're in town again. Use my private number that I gave you.

Ever your friend,
Sinclair

January 7, 1948

My darling,

I cannot endure being separated from you another minute. Do you know how much I love you? I am despondent living without you. I cannot go on this way. I now know and fully understand that you cannot … will not … leave your present situation.

Sinclair

I unfolded the newspaper clipping dated January 31, 1948.

WASHINGTON: Senator Sinclair Dobbs died at his home in Arlington, Virginia of unknown causes. His illustrious career spanned two administrations as right-hand man to Presidents Roosevelt and Truman. He ran for office and instantaneously became a Senate leader representing Tennessee. He leaves his wife, Estelle, and three adult children.

I had stumbled into a world beyond my years.

Fearful I might get caught holding these strange writings, I tied the ribbon loosely back around the letters, tucking the newspaper clipping into the packet. Then I put everything back into the shoebox. With my heart racing, I placed the shoebox on the shelf, stuffed behind "Parcheesi" and a stack of other games no one played anymore.

Two weeks later, what I had read still troubled me. When no one was around, I crept down to the playroom, stood before the wall lined with oak cabinets, took a deep breath, and opened a door. I knelt down and frantically pulled out the games, one by one, piling them on the floor. Nothing was left on the shelf. Empty. The shoebox was gone.

• FOREST LEGACY •

Frannie may not have fully grasped the significance of her marrying Hans W. Nolde, son of hosiery baron, industrialist, inventor, and environmentalist Jacob Nolde (1859-1916). For all her intellect, how could she foresee that the legendary forest and successful hosiery business might strain what appeared to be an idyllic relationship? How could she foresee that her flying might become a wedge? Becoming a pilot, playing a key role in WWII, and then becoming a Civil Air Patrol colonel were crazy ideas when she and Hans pledged "… for better, for worse…."

Her notoriety as a mother of seven who became a WWII pilot reflected her lack of interest in land conservation and a family heritage related to the Nolde Forest. However, Hans did focus on continuing Jacob's legacy, until he ran out of money and energy. Her interest lay elsewhere.

How much of the Nolde history did she know? A simple inventor and lover of German pine forests, patriarch Jacob Nolde was a straightforward, humble man, who didn't hold illusions of grandeur or exhibit airs. He demanded none from others.

In 1888, just eight years after leaving Germany, Jacob Nolde invited Henry Lorah and George Horst to form Nolde & Horst, a manufacturing company that grew into one of the largest knitting mills in Pennsylvania. Jacob was an imaginative inventor who returned to Germany to study how to design weaving machines that would propel the business to become the main competitor of Berkshire Knitting Mills, an outfit many times the size of Nolde & Horst.

To meet manufacturing demands, Jacob didn't allow Hans to continue at Franklin and Marshall College after freshman year, insisting he work at Nolde & Horst. Thus, Hans had no chance to discover who he was or to develop the part of oneself that yearns for expression. Perhaps that explains the anger and disappointment that lived under the surface in Hans' life and occasionally erupted. How ironic that Frannie's father had pulled her from Oberlin.

As Jacob developed his business, he dreamed about creating a German pine forest modeled after the "princely" coniferous forests of his native Westphalia. He said he wanted to create "the most beautiful pine forest in Pennsylvania." Inspired by the sight of a single white pine, he purchased 500 acres outside the city. Later he added roughly another 155 acres, and with recent donations, the total is 725 acres. After planting thousands of trees in formal Germanic rows, Jacob hired an expert to manage the forest.

COMMONWEALTH OF PENNSYLVANIA
DEPARTMENT OF ENVIRONMENTAL RESOURCES
HARRISBURG, PENNSYLVANIA 17120
THE STORY OF
THE NOLDE FOREST
A
SINGLE
WHITE
PINE

When Jacob died in 1916, the logical person to take Jacob's place was his son Hans, who secured the property by buying out his siblings' shares. Hans continued to oversee the development of the forestry plans.

In his book about Punches Run, *A Single White Pine,* Hans' eldest son John writes:

> *After 1934, the number of seedlings planted was drastically reduced. Again, this may have been because the major task had been completed. But it is probably no coincidence that the drop in activity coincided with the onset of the Depression of the 1930s and the general economic dislocations of World War II and the postwar years.*

To his credit, Hans oversaw the planting of 1,500,000 pine and hundreds of hardwood trees. The forest thrived.

Jacob exhibited love for the land and the animals that lived on it. Hans felt a strong pull to preserve his father's legacy as both a forester and woodsman. He added to the property the beautiful castle as a family home. But despite his effort to ensure the future of "The Place" for generations to come, Hans lost the creativity or drive to develop Punches Run much beyond basic maintenance by workers who came and went. And Hans didn't think of establishing an endowment to ensure fiscal security for "The Place." Overwhelmed by business, family, and Punches Run obligations, he was unable to do justice to any.

Nevertheless, Hans had preserved Jacob's dream, and it has become a priceless gift to Pennsylvania. Many environmentalists and state forestry personnel have come to examine the property, learn the planting techniques and species, emulate the progressive steps, plant similar types of trees, and follow Jacob's methods for forest management. Punches Run gained great respect.

Pennsylvania bought the property in the '60s and converted Hans' family mansion into the Nolde Forest Environmental Education Center. In 1970, "The Place" opened as the Nolde State Forest.

• WYOMING •

Daddy responded to the challenges in his business and marriage by turning to his tennis partnership with a spinster, Sidney Kutz. For many years, he and Sidney won the Reading Country Club mixed doubles tournament. As emcee at the tournament dinner, he would say a few words in somewhat slurred speech, and then the audience would insist he sing Roy Rogers' song "Why, Oh Why, Did I Ever Leave Wyoming?" When he finished, his fellow tennis players and friends would egg him on to sing it again. He had a pretty good voice.

Daddy held Wyoming close to his heart. Without Mother, he spent many summers there, often taking his children. As I grew up, I went three times; the last was after I graduated from high school, and Daddy and I drove out with my cousin, Charlie Guthrie. Daddy had bought property on White Grass Ranch in Moose, Wyoming, right in the middle of Jackson Hole. From the cabin, we looked up at the three grand peaks of the Tetons.

Whenever he arrived out West, Daddy became a changed man — deliriously happy, the happiest I'd ever known him. He quickly donned his bolo necktie, cowboy boots, and Stetson, and mounted a horse for a ride over the plains and into the mountains. Nothing could take away his feeling of contentment.

Mother had no interest in Wyoming, and she never accompanied him. They had nothing to share in this environment. Had she cared for this side of him, I believe they might have repaired their relationship when it became rocky.

My parents gradually grew apart. Different interests. Different energies. Different visions of how and where to live.

And so, Daddy began to spend time with his golf partner, Kit Brown — the "Widow Brown." Many years later, he divorced Mother and married Kit. Kit, however, was not a horseback rider, so she didn't like the Wyoming Daddy loved and insisted upon his leaving the Tetons for a place in Arizona, where they could play golf year-round. Daddy caved in.

When older, I realized I needed to "drink in" Wyoming as if it were Daddy's soul and total being. Returning to Jackson Hole as an adult, I yearned to put my feet on the soil he loved. I made this connection with him so that I wouldn't feel bereft from his abandonment. I found ways to heal that wound in Wyoming.

• BEACH HAVEN •

Instead of heading for Wyoming, Mother took us every year to Beach Haven, New Jersey, for our annual month of summer vacation at the shore. We rented the same place and walked to the same beach every day. This was a favorite family time for Chris and me, with our older siblings coming when they could. The place smelled of musty salt water, with plenty of sand underfoot. We went to the beach as a group of kids, with cousins and family friends who were also vacationing. Mother rarely accompanied us, unless the younger ones had no chaperone. Otherwise, what she did to pass the time of day remains a mystery to me.

When I was around eight, Daddy arrived for his usual summer weekend. One evening, at a large cocktail party with children included, Daddy said he had someone special he wanted me to meet. My sense of danger felt like an electric shock when I saw his impish look of joy, as it told me he liked this person very much. He introduced me to a smiling, strange woman. I knew something was out of place, but I couldn't figure it out. I forgot about the meeting until years later. I wondered: Had he introduced me to Kit that summer? She had been married twice before, divorcing her first husband because he had no money, gossipers said, and driving her second husband to suicide, the same gossipers said. I imagine Mother wanted to believe the stories about Kit because she began to call Kit the "Black Widow" and so did Sally, Chris, and I.

CHAPTER NINE

The Wartime Mill

• "E" FOR "EXCELLENCE" •

Frannie was smarter than Hans. I imagine that got in their way. While she overshadowed him intellectually, I never heard her humiliate, patronize, or mock him. Nevertheless, during the war, she could have run Nolde & Horst, manufacturing socks, gloves, and mittens for troops along with secret wartime parts; and after the war, she could have rescued the company when it started to lose ground.

Soon after Pearl Harbor, the government told the company to shift emphasis from hosiery to military production. As secretary / treasurer, Daddy worked with Nolde & Horst management to make the change productive and effective.

For designing and producing millions of cushion-soled socks, woolen gloves, and mittens, Nolde & Horst received the Army-Navy "E" Award for giving excellent comfort and warmth to infantry soldiers as well as for making significant parts for ships and planes. In a 1944 ceremony honoring the employees and management, Brigadier General Roland Walsh presented the award to the president of Nolde & Horst, John H. Vogt. A brass band played, dignitaries spoke, and each employee received an "E" pin for "Excellence."

The program cited Nolde & Horst as being among the first American companies to convert to wartime production. It also summarized Jacob Nolde's contribution to the early days of manufacturing hosiery. He had built a large, well-equipped machine shop to both construct and maintain elaborate looms. General Walsh praised the company for its wartime "products of the machine shop" — secret "war ordinance materials" significant to the war effort: pullies and links for the Air Corps and Navy, and "fuse adapters for bombs."

THE NOLDE & HORST COMPANY

The Nolde and Horst Company, Reading's Pioneer Hosiery Producer, Utilizes Machine Shop to Turn Out War Ordnance Materials

Company Also Produces "Cushion Sole" Socks and Gloves for the Armed Forces

• EXCELLENCE FALTERS •

At the end of the war, Hans had withstood family lobbying and intrigue to become president of Nolde & Horst, ousting President Vogt. He won that skirmish, but the next test was a huge challenge. The war had ended, and he needed to return the knitting mill to its original status as a premier hosiery company. That proved more difficult than Hans anticipated as he struggled to find the money and technical help to turn the machine shop and the looms back to pre-war production and peace-time products. Nolde & Horst began to lose its edge.

With Hans as president, the company attempted to resurrect interest in Nolde products: elasticized three-inch-wide belts in a variety of colors, nylons in many shades, men's socks, woolen gloves, and variations on items they'd made for soldiers. Nothing took hold.

His competition, Berkshire Knitting Mills, was more facile and beat him to it. Nolde & Horst no longer was a top-ranking manufacturer. As the company began to falter, so did Hans. He acted as if he had either lost interest or never had the capability to keep the business afloat.

He played backgammon at the Wyomissing Club most afternoons. More and more frequently, he ignored his business responsibilities. Was his behavior an unconscious indication of denial? Or was he projecting manliness, strutting around and smoking cigars to distract people from the scent of loss and incompetence? Was he joined by Kit to enjoy those afternoons of play and frolic? Mother certainly did not accompany him. I still wonder what went on.

• ADDICTIONS •

Hans and Frannie continued to throw their large cocktail parties. Without question, heavy smoking and heavy drinking were a constant part of this lavish life. That combination took its toll on our family. Bobby was the first: She died in her early 50s from tongue cancer. Jake died in his early 60s. Jeanne also died in her early 60s of emphysema. When Sally's second husband, Tom, died in an accident, leaving her with two small children, she turned to alcohol for solace. After living into her 70s, Sally's body was riddled with cancer. The pattern had been set by Mother and Daddy who had their own issues with alcohol and cigarettes, even though Daddy advocated "moderation." They were hooked and couldn't control their excesses. Mother had a constitution that tolerated continual abuse from smoking and alcohol, but Daddy didn't have the fortitude and eventually succumbed. Somehow Johnny, Chris, and I avoided addiction, not drawn to smoking or drinking. The worries and woes of a failing business affected Hans' health and relationship with Frannie. As Hans' star was receding, Frannie's was rising with international publicity for her flying achievements.

Hans was forced to sell the company in 1951. After the sale, he filled his time with two ventures: making charcoal and raising pheasants. Neither became a financial success, each only a hobby.

Concerning their marriage, other early warning signs set off alarms for those who noticed. Sometimes Daddy didn't come home at night. One evening when I was ten, I ran up the spiral staircase to find Mother standing at the top of the landing, crying. Daddy hadn't come home yet, and it was late, well after dinner. I asked her what was wrong and why she was crying. She said, "Nothing, dear. I'm crying because I'm so happy." I slowly walked to my room, pondering why someone cried when happy.

As a young girl who heard bits and pieces but not the whole story, my confusion created heartache for me. But Mother's heartache must have been immense because she knew the whole story.

When Daddy became president of Nolde & Horst, he also began to experience heart problems. His first heart attack convinced him to stop smoking. He took to holding an unlit cigarette in his mouth until it became soggy. Soon, he turned to clenching his empty cigarette holder between his teeth for a stale taste of tobacco. In 1958, another heart attack kept him from my wedding. An eighth attack took his life in 1965 at the age of 69.

PART FOUR

Pilot

CIVIL
U.S.A.F.
AUXILIARY
AIR PATROL

CHAPTER TEN

Aviatrix: Through a Child's Eyes

• MOTHER FLIES •

At the age of 39, with a brood of seven children, from little ones to young adults, Mother began flying lessons. She quickly progressed from qualifying for a private pilot's license, to an instructor's license, a commercial pilot's license, and, finally, an instrument rating for bad-weather flying because few airports had control towers with personnel to help small planes in inclement weather. Each license required numerous solo hours and demanding exams.

In the summer of 1941, I was four-and-a-half. Every morning, I climbed onto the radiator in Jake's room to look out the window to watch Mother get into her black Buick convertible with red leather seats and slowly gain momentum around the front circle to drive off. While I cried and called for her not to go, no one heard me or responded to my tears. She was on her way to the Reading airport. Each day was the same: I feared she would not return, and when she came home at night, I knew I would have to watch her leave again. It took me months to outgrow the pain.

When WWII prompted gas rationing, Mother soon stopped driving her Buick and bought a flashy motor scooter with a sidecar. For the ride to the airport, she changed from stylish clothes and high heels to sporty herringbone tweeds and houndstooth, sensible brown leather shoes, and warm jackets. We begged and pestered her to ride in the sidecar, and sometimes she gave in. One day, with no one riding

Reading Times

Associated Press United Press AP Wirephoto International News

READING, PA., SATURDAY MORNING, SEPTEMBER 18, 1943

Reading's Flying Grandmother Commands CAP Sta
Hopes Seven Children Will Learn to Follow Sky Tr

Mrs. Frances Nolde Sees Women's Place As Plane Pilots

By MARC RUTNER

"My one regret is that I didn't learn to fly 20 years ago."

That, in one brief sentence, is the complete sentiment of the first woman to be appointed station-commander of a flying unit.

Mrs. Frances Nolde, of "Punches Run," Sheerlund, Reading, companion, friend, mother, playmate of "the Nolde children," seven of them, and recently a grandmother, learned to fly at the age of 39. Two years later, on June 27, 1943, she was selected as commander of the Reading Courier Station No. 4, Pennsylvania Wing, CAP, replacing Capt. Carl Reber, who is now adjutant of the Pennsylvania Wing, stationed at headquarters in Harrisburg.

She first learned to fly at the Reading Municipal Airport as a challenge "that age had nothing to do with ability to fly," she said, and is happy that more women today are proving their place in what had once been solely man's domain of the skies.

She is more than pleased with her new job for, as she pointed out, after Pearl Harbor she realized that the demand on manpower for the flying forces would seriously curtail operation of commercial flying firms and she is determined to establish woman's place in that field of aviation. She sees no reason why women cannot take the place of pilots who have gone into active service, as has been done by other women entering the various services to replace enlisted men who had been detailed to desk work.

Sees Place for Women

Having learned to fly herself, Mrs. Nolde is convinced that what one or two women did in past years, larger groups of women can do today. She illustrated by citing what girls who graduated from Texas schools are doing by flying twin-engined planes after 150 hours of training.

As commander of the station adjacent to the Reading Army Airfield, Mrs. Nolde, with the rating of second lieutenant, has seven assistants; one regular pilot, Lieut. Francis Bachman, who alternates flying duties with her; five auxil-[illegible]ots; and Joseph Zaffiro, of

Relaxing from her executive and flying duties for the CAP Industrial Courier Service, Mrs. Frances Nolde (upper left panel), first woman to be appointed commander of the local station, No. 4, Pennsylvania Wing, spends all her free time with Hans Christopher, 8 (on floor), looking at his model plane; Frances Dean, 6 (on right), reading a story to her, while Jacob, 15, adjusts the lamp behind [illegible] right panel shows Mrs.

Posing for the Reading Times, *Chris plays with a plane, Mother and Francie read, and Jake turns on the light.*

shotgun in her sidecar, she skidded over trolley tracks, flew over the handlebars, and cut up her knees and those tweeds. She never rode the scooter again.

Mother soon became the American woman with the most solo hours: 600. By the end of her career, newspapers said Frannie had clocked over 10,000 solo hours, a number that may be an exaggeration, but it does appear in the Congressional Record.

Mother referred to her first flying lesson in several newspaper articles. In 1951, she told *The Binghamton Sun* that she was so bad, it "almost finished me." She continued, "I was frightened. One look at the instrument panel convinced me that I would never get to know the altimeter from the fuel gauge. The instructor bet one of his friends I would never take another lesson. But I was determined not to let it get me down. I turned up right on time for the next lesson, and from then it was clear sailing."

Mother looked at flying as a "basic skill" everyone should have. She believed she had to keep one step ahead of her children, whom she was convinced would all learn to fly. And she said flying soon became "like a disease." She was addicted.

She insisted that a well-maintained plane was safer than any car, and that pilot error was invariably the reason for an airplane accident.

When I was sitting in her co-pilot seat one day, I asked what she would do if the engine conked out. Over the engine's hum, she calmly replied she constantly watched for landing sites: a meadow, a strip of unused land, railroad tracks, even a long, straight road. From then on, I looked for landing spots, too.

At the beginning of her flying career, Frannie wrote a letter to *The Reading Eagle's* society editor, Lilly March, about learning to fly and getting her license.

As Seen by Her

By Lilly March | 10-14-41

With deep gratitude I hand over this space today to Mrs. Hans W. Nolde, who has lately added airplane piloting to her already incredibly long list of accomplishments and who explains why in the following entertaining and instructive letter.

Dear Lilly:

You asked me WHY I was learning to fly. If you had told me two or three months ago that I'd be flying a plane ALONE, over Reading today, I'd have said it was a fantasy. But your question set me to thinking, and then to wondering if I could explain "learning to fly" on a purely logical basis.

When my children take up flying, as I am sure they will do some day, I want to be flying with them rather than sitting at home worrying about them. I have to do it now, while I still possess a tiny bit of courage.

And speaking of courage, it really requires very little of that — once the initial hurdle of making up one's mind is accomplished. During my first lesson, I was extremely nervous — because of what I DIDN'T know about flying. I looked upon my instructor as some kind of daredevil who was impervious to all danger and without regard for his life — as well as mine. When he told me to pull the stick gently toward me and note how the plane began to climb, or gain altitude, my hands began to perspire and that half-minute seemed interminable. I didn't realize that he could have instantly corrected any mistake I might make. Then, when we had resumed a level course, he showed me how to make a turn to the left — by applying a little pressure on the left pedal, and simultaneously pushing the stick to the left. At that point, I resolved to turn myself over to a psychiatrist if I was lucky enough to ever get safely back on the ground.

I had signed up for the "solo course," which means you will have as many lessons as you need in order to be able to solo, or fly alone. If it ever happened, it would surely be the ultimate and final goal for me.

The first solo flight is something remembered forever. I can't put into words the utter aloneness that engulfs your whole being when your instructor gets out of the plane and says, "It's all yours — take it away." You desperately want to implore him to go up with you "just one more time." But you know that he would never be sending you up alone if he weren't dead sure you were capable of doing it.

You have discovered that your instructor is anything from a daredevil you thought when he gave you the controls for the first time. He is a sound person, with years of flying experience, a level head, and a great amount of caution thrown in. So you muster a smile and wave a hand that you hope isn't shaking too noticeably — you open the throttle and before you know it, you are down the runway, you are in the air, climbing to 400 feet. You make a 90-degree left turn, then another, following a rectangular course around the field. It's time to cut your motor and make your approach for a landing. And as you are landing, you see him standing there watching you. Suddenly you decide you'll show him you're really not scared at all. So you open the throttle again and sail down the runway for a second takeoff — you know that never again in your whole life will you feel QUITE as you did on that first solo takeoff. Then you buy everyone in the office a coke, and they all congratulate you, and you suddenly realize how simple it all was.

Now, the most amazing realization happens. Being able to solo, which was just a remote possibility, has actually occurred. As the exuberance begins to subside, it dawns on you that thousands of other people have soloed. You are a rank amateur who doesn't know a blessed thing about flying. You dash back to the airport to find out how many solo hours are required and whatever else must be accomplished in order to get a private pilot's license. When you learn that it is 35 solo hours, plus passing a flight test that includes spins and precision landings, plus passing a written examination in meteorology and navigation, you buy all the books and sign up for a ground course in these subjects. Lilly, I must tell you that I'm afraid there is no end to this. There is a much-coveted commercial license — there is an instrument rating — there is night-flying, and heaven knows what else. And as Scarlett O'Hara always said, "I'll think of that tomorrow" — and I'm afraid I will.

— Affectionately yours, F.W.N.

When in the air, Frannie said she was "in heaven," often alone, in total repose, with all the household worries far below. While she often said she learned to fly in order to surpass her father's accomplishments in racing pacers, or to keep up with her children who were sure to become pilots, she finally admitted she loved being in the sky as a peaceful relief from the melee of seven children. The reasons didn't matter: She had found her place in the blue skies.

It wasn't long before I begged Mother to take me up to experience aerobatics: inside and outside loops, barrel rolls, stall turns, and lazy eights my brother Chris had told me about. It never happened, because the only trick she was willing to perform was to dive, stall, and restart the engine — but not with me. Her reluctance made my flights with her all the more precious. How well I remember my anticipation as I sat by the runway tarmac, waiting to fly with Mother.

Much to my surprise and Mother's, I soon realized that flying made me air sick. The fumes from the gas and oil in the cockpit, mixed with Mother's cigarette smoke, upset my stomach. To solve the problem, Mother gave me the co-pilot's seat, and made Chris sit in the back; he wasn't happy. But sitting up front didn't help so I

Waiting patiently to fly with Mother

screwed up my courage and begged her not to smoke. She took my plea seriously and stopped smoking in the cockpit. From then on, I loved flying with Mother. Mother taught us the rudiments of flying. When I turned the wheel to the left, the plane banked to the left. When I pushed the wheel forward, the nose went down. When I pulled the wheel back toward me, the nose turned upward. Mother exclaimed, "Look, Tunie! You're flying!"

Eventually, Mother flew Chris and me to boarding school in Connecticut, and she later flew me to a school interview in Andover, Massachusetts. Churning 50-mile-an-hour winds frightened me and stunned the headmistress who picked us up at a little airport. Nonplussed, Mother shrugged off the winds.

The next fall, I went to that school, Abbot Academy, despite my misgivings about it being an all-girls school. When I graduated a few years later, the whole school gathered outside ready to march to the baccalaureate service, seniors first, in their caps and gowns.

Mother was late. Her solution was to buzz the school, circling very low several times and tipping her wings to salute the occasion. Despite my embarrassment, students and faculty cheered and waved at her as she flew by. Oh, Mother!

When I was a teenager, a return flight to Washington was terrifying, as my head repeatedly hit the cockpit roof while Mother prepared for landing about a mile behind a jet airliner. For the first time, she was learning how forceful jet exhaust could be. Those episodes demanded skillful flying maneuvers for which she became well known. They were also more than enough to stop my asking for aerobatic tricks.

With all seven of us growing up, off to boarding school or college, Mother went to the airport as if it were her day job, a place where everyone knew her. Although I was her youngest child, she rarely visited me in boarding school, so I was thrilled when she flew to Connecticut to see me in our fifth-grade play when I was ten. As an adult, I wrote this semi-fictional vignette about Mother's visit:

Broken Wing

Leaning against the hanger door, the airport owner saw the small plane two miles out, heading in at 45 degrees downwind. Because there was no control tower, he knew the pilot would be broadcasting the plane's location and status to nearby pilots in order to clear the area. Not long after, the plane circled wide overhead, throttled back to 1800 RPM, flaps dropping gradually from 10 to 20, and finally to 30 degrees on final approach, right in the slot. Steadily descending to 800 feet above ground at midfield, the plane landed with speed under control.

"Smooth and gradual, without a bump," he thought. The silver Navion taxied up alongside "Bamboo Baby," a yellow Cessna, and parked. The circling propeller slowed to a stop while the engine revved up, then cut out with sputtering coughs.

A hand in a red deerskin glove slid the canopy back. A slender, silk-clad leg swung out as a red leather pump descended onto the low-slung wing. A woman's lithe body emerged, dressed in a sharkskin suit with a fur wrapped around her neck, its fox mouth clipped to its tail. She reached into the back seat for the handle of her red leather hatbox.

After securing the cockpit, she stood for a moment on the wing of her plane. Placing her gloved hand over her eyes, she scanned the tarmac. She exhaled when she saw the Highland Taxi on the other side of the fence. Turning her body to place a shapely foot on the lower step, she raised her skirt and hopped down.

The owner loped out from the shadows of the hanger, curly hair askew, and smiled. "Beautiful landing. What can I do for you?" He reached for the wooden blocks lying on the ground and pushed them up against the front wheels.

She stopped, turned, and smoothed her skirt. His eyes met hers. In a honey voice she replied, "Why, thank you. My next leg is a four-hour flight. I'm going into town now, but I shan't be long. Would you mind filling up the two tanks? And looking under the cowling? Thanks."

He held her stare. "I'll … I'll fill it up right away. Sure that's all?" She nodded, handed him the keys, and thanked him again with an enigmatic smile. A flush crept up his neck to his cheeks as he watched her striding toward the fence, stopping once, to turn and carefully straighten the seams of her stockings.

The ride to her daughter's school took about 20 minutes. With hatbox and pocketbook over one arm, she paid the taxi driver and told him to return at noon. She looked up at the three-story Tudor hall and shivered slightly.

She hurried through the damp, gray vestibule, pushed open the heavy oaken door, and entered. She stood at one end of a long, paneled living room. Her eyes scanned the room, lingering on the stage, a converted staircase landing. She noted children's laughter and the bustle of people seating themselves. Her eyes also caught the frame of a tall, well-groomed gentleman dressed in a camel's hair jacket and paisley tie. He acknowledged her glance with glistening eyes, and approached her. "I see you made it. That's wonderful. I hope you enjoy your visit with your daughter."

She swept a lock of hair back from her face and met his eyes. "Thank you. I'm sure I will."

She slid into an end seat in the last row, sensing turned heads and eyes upon her. With a hint of a smile, she crossed her legs, pulled off her gloves, finger by finger, and settled into the chair.

"Oh, Mother, you're here!" She stood to receive her daughter who bounded out and flung her arms around her mother's waist. "Oh, Mother, I have so much to tell you. You have to stay forever. Please don't leave."

"Of course, dear heart. Now tell me about the play."

"It's about a dream I had, just before coming home for Christmas. The story's about … um, I better not spoil it. Is that all right?"

"Of course, dear heart. I can't wait!" She laughed as she squeezed her daughter once more. The girl dashed back to the dressing room, long blonde braids flying behind.

The school children sitting near the woman squirmed and talked animatedly. She tapped her red nails against her leg. Finally, the man in the camel's hair jacket rose and turned, stilling the audience. "You are about to see a one-act play called "Broken Wing," written and produced by our fifth grade. The idea came from a fifth-grader's dream about birds. The class decided to study birds and then create this play. Please welcome the fifth-grade players."

Her fingers politely patted her palm as applause encouraged the children to come on stage. The room lights went down with the sounds of birdsong. Stage lights illumminated a forest scene. Three bright yellow American Goldfinches flew in, darting up and down. Two Robin Redbreasts hopped alongside three red-and-black Scarlet Tanagers, dipping their wings. Two Indigo Buntings flapped their wings, followed by three swooping Baltimore Orioles. All the birds stopped to listen to the Oriole's clear, whistle-like song. Then a lone Bluebird, with long blonde braids peeking out, hobbled to the middle of the forest, her wing in a sling.

Robin hopped to the side of the broken bird. "Oh, Bluebird, I'm sorry you've been so badly hurt by the storm. You must be in great pain."

Baltimore Orioles swooped over to them. "All our nests are destroyed and so are our feeding places. What will we do?"

The birds clasped wing ends and flew around the forest, singing in unison, "What will we do? What will we do?"

Scarlet Tanager said, "Stop. We know what to do. After all, we are the remarkable and extraordinary bird nation."

The play went on, with friendly birds administering aid to Bluebird, who prompted them to build a first aid center for other wounded birds to help them find a new way of life.

Close to the finale, Bluebird's mother caught her daughter sneaking a look, to see if she was enjoying herself. Then Bluebird's mother fingered her diamond and ruby rings, moved to the edge of her seat. She looked at her watch and discretely slipped her hands back into her gloves, pushing against the fingers until they were snug. Gathering her hatbox and pocketbook, she kept her eyes on the stage. She slid off the chair and tiptoed to the door. She heard applause. Looking back, she saw the birds taking a curtain call. She stepped out the door. The taxi was waiting.

CHAPTER ELEVEN

Responding to War

• NEW COMMITMENTS •

In 1938, Frannie and Hans visited Germany, where Frannie saw groups of farmers marching in the fields in military formation with pitchforks over their shoulders, as if they were holding rifles. When Frannie returned, she told friends that Germany was preparing for war. When Japan attacked Pearl Harbor on December 7, 1941, America declared war, and Frannie quickly stopped flying for pleasure and began flying for a cause. She was now flying to help defeat the Germans who produced beautiful pine forests and helped invent innovative machinery for manufacturing hosiery. But German culture was her husband's heritage, not hers.

The airport that Hans and his business friends had founded in the 1920s became the lodestar for Frannie's career in aviation. Hans had encouraged her to begin flying lessons, not knowing her success would overshadow his.

Once Frannie became a committed pilot, Hans bought her a two-seater Piper Cub Coupe, then replaced it with another. When Frannie became a wartime Civil Air Patrol courier, Hans gave her a Fairchild 24, a large four-seater.

• CIVIL AIR PATROL •

Early in 1942, Frannie joined the Civil Air Patrol (CAP) as a charter member of Reading Squadron 22. In October, she became Reading's CAP courier commander, part of Pennsylvania's "wing." Frannie was the first woman in the nation to hold such a position.

While some people thought civilian aviation should be shut down for fear of sabotage, military and civilian aviators formed the CAP to support the war effort. CAP pilots provided border and coastal patrols, military assistance and pilot training, courier service and cargo transportation, and search and rescue operations.

With the help of the Army Air Corps and the initiative of President Roosevelt's Director of the Office of Civilian Defense Fiorello La Guardia, Civil Air Patrol was put to work. By the end of the war, CAP pilots had flown over 500,000 mission hours. Ninety aircraft were lost and 65 pilots were killed, including 26 while on coastal patrol.

A CAP newsletter called *Keystone Wing Slip* describes Frannie's work:

> In October 1942 the Reading PA Courier Station No. 4 was born.... Fourteen defense plants signed a contract for the service, ... [and] Lieutenant Frances Nolde [soon] took over command.... In the first year they completed 295 flights for a total of 480 hours of flying time, carrying 2,229,770 pounds of vital cargo. The cargo consisted of pressed steel engine parts, mining equipment, parachute thread, gas-mask cement, steel castings, ammunition item samples, lathe replacement parts, and countless other materials that helped speed the war effort along. Passenger miles [added] 19,448 [to cargo] miles . . . for a total of 37,700.

> Often CAP courier trips would take two days, but there were times when it was a short hop. For example, a steel company needed small bolts in order to continue work on the production line. After locating the bolts in a nearby factory, they called the courier service. Twenty-five minutes later the CAP plane landed at a nearby airport, picked up the bolts, and delivered them to the production line, using an auto at the end, all in less than an hour's time.
>
> Lieutenant Nolde used her roomy four-place Fairchild 24 on many flights. ... Lt. Nolde has been working seven days a week, between flying and keeping the logs, records, and ledger books up to date. A great many shipments of gun castings have been flown to the Bell Aircraft factory at Buffalo.
>
> ...Emergency calls are frequent. A short time ago a truck strike in New England held up the delivery of rayon for a parachute plant working on government contracts against a deadline. Reading Courier dispatched three airplanes to Manchester, Vermont, bringing back about 1700 pounds of rayon. Two additional flights the following day brought back enough to keep the production line going until the strike was settled and the usual flow of material was available.

In 1943, *The Reading Times* featured Frannie's budding career as a CAP airport commander. The headline reads: "Reading's Flying Grandmother Commands CAP Station. Hopes Seven Children will learn to follow Sky Trails. Mrs. Frances Nolde Sees Women's Place as Plane Pilots." The article begins with her saying, "My one regret is that I didn't learn to fly 20 years ago."

> That, in one brief sentence, is the complete sentiment of the first woman to be appointed station-commander of a flying unit, Mrs. Frances Nolde. ... She is happy that more women today are proving their place in what had been solely man's domain of the skies.

She is more than pleased with her new job for, as she pointed out, after Pearl Harbor she realized that the demand on manpower for the flying forces would seriously curtail operation of commercial flying firms, and she is determined to establish women's place in that field of aviation. She sees no reason why women cannot take the place of pilots who have gone into active service, as has been done by other women entering various services to replace enlisted men who had been detailed to desk work.

Having learned to fly herself, Mrs. Nolde is convinced that what one or two women did in past years, larger groups of women can do today. She illustrated this by citing what girls who graduated from Texas schools are doing by flying twin-engine planes after 130 hours of training.

Frannie told *The Reading Eagle:*

"...The greatest service we offer to a defense plant is speed — speed in carrying vital materials to and from a production line, often saving several days or even a week's production by getting necessary material or a piece of machinery to a plant."

While explaining how they sometimes branch out from being an auxiliary of the Army, she recounted a story about a Navy officer who missed his train in Reading, while en route home on a 48-hour furlough, the first he had had in 18 months. "It was one of those days," Mrs. Nolde smiled, "when the birds were walking, as the saying goes. The airport at his home town was only a small rough field. We got off all right, but it was rough over the mountains."

After the worst of the trip was over, Mrs. Nolde asked the Navy man if he had not been disturbed by the rough weather on his first flight and by a pilot of whom he knew nothing. He just said, "Lady, I've been on a sub-chaser for a year and a half, and if this is the toughest spot I get myself into, I'll be very lucky."

She smiled reminiscently. "The joy and happiness of his wife and two children at the airport was more than ample reward for a rather rough journey."

Frannie's compassion for the sailor and his family speaks to how women sometimes changed the tone and atmosphere of war. Frannie said that to become a pilot took more than courage. She believed the mind had to be conditioned not to believe flying was a hazardous undertaking.

The interview concludes, "Eventually, Mrs. Nolde hopes all the children will learn to fly. She looks toward the day when the sky above Punches Run will roar with the motors of eight planes, in formation, and silhouetting Sheerlund, with their wings."

The Reading Eagle reported that the Reading CAP courier service was the only one to continue operation throughout the war. Frannie deserves credit for that accomplishment.

Captain Frances Nolde

• RELATIONSHIP •

Before the war ended, many aspects of Hans and Frannie's marriage began to quietly shift, unraveling what they had created. Frannie was now flying Hans to Washington to fulfill his volunteer job at the Office of Price Administration (OPA), a key part of Franklin Roosevelt's Second New Deal. Hans became a special consultant on hosiery to the Consumer Goods Division, committing to a six-month term, ending in February 1944.

He wrote his eldest son Johnny, "It is not the kind of job I like nor according to my training and experience; however, I shall see it through." He couldn't afford to take much time off from a business that had rapidly shifted to critical and secret wartime production.

Hans wrote again to Johnny, expressing signs of a strain in Hans and Frannie's marriage. Hans ended the letter by saying, "I am trying to wean Mother away from her war efforts to take a week off, but you know how she feels. We won't be able to take Rome unless she stays on her job."

Frannie was working seven days a week, nonstop. After the war, her obsession with aviation did not end, and Frannie soon achieved international acclaim as a famous pilot.

CHAPTER TWELVE

Powder Puff Derby

Today, if an all-women's transcontinental airplane race were called a "Powder Puff Derby," the organizer would be run out of town as a misogynist. But in 1948, when Frannie won the race, the women most likely smiled politely and brushed off the frivolous connotation of "Powder Puff."

Horse races and air races were manly pursuits called "derbies," in which only men could be jockeys or pilots. But in 1929, less than ten years after American women gained the vote, they held their first all-women's air derby. Amelia Earhart, Pancho Barnes, Louise Thaden, and other women aviators raced from Santa Monica, California, to Cleveland, Ohio.

As part of that significant event, Amelia Earhart invited a group of women pilots to stand under the wings of planes in Cleveland to represent a powerful female force. Named for its 99 charter members, it became "The Ninety-Nines International Organization of Women Pilots." The Ninety-Nines continues to this day to promote the advancement of women's aviation through education and scholarships, and to share women's passion for flying. And as Amelia said, "For the fun of it."

After winning the Powder Puff Derby, Frannie became an active member of the Ninety-Nines, a governor as well as vice-president of its contest division.

Amelia Earhart, circa 1930

Despite the success of the 1929 Powder Puff Derby, most men and women did not take women pilots seriously, thinking women could never be as capable as male pilots. Early female pilots constantly had to prove themselves in air shows and short races. To promote sales, airplane manufacturers sometimes gave women pilots planes that weren't fit for demanding races. Crashes in these sub-standard planes renewed the prejudice against female flyers. It was a slow, long journey to approval.

Eventually, women were allowed to compete in major races but in divisions separate from men. As women gained racing experience, they proved themselves by achieving times and speeds equal to those of men. Women's races continued through the 1930s, stopped during WWII, and resumed in 1947 with the All-Women's Transcontinental Air Race, still nicknamed "Powder Puff Derby."

In 1948 and 1949, the races were sponsored by Frannie's rival, Jacqueline Cochran, a prominent pilot with financial means and connections. Members of the Ninety-Nines Los Angeles Chapter drafted the first formal set of rules and regulations for women's air racing and developed an official time-keeping system, more reliable than the original honor-based system, with safety a priority. The Powder Puff Derby became a well-recognized event, with its own headquarters, executive secretary, and board of directors to prepare each race. The message was clear: Women fly as fast and skillfully as men.

• FRANNIE COMPETES •

In 1948, after flying for seven years, Frannie decided to enter the Powder Puff Derby. She had become so well-known as an outstanding pilot that the manufacturer of the Ryan Navion hoped to promote sales by asking Frannie to race their newest single-engine plane 2,540 miles from Palm Springs, California, to Miami, Florida. She was thrilled to see the inscription on the side: "Ryan Navion, Aviation Consultants, Inc., Reading, PA," as she had become the Consultants' director of public relations.

Sleek, with low-slung wings, the maroon plane overshadowed the others with its power and maneuverability.

She Won!

Frannie wrote a journal describing her experience, beginning:

> On Saturday, May 29th, I taxied out to the runway on Lindbergh Field at San Diego, California. It was a brand new Ryan Navion I had picked up at the factory — a shiny deep maroon one — and my heart began to beat a little faster as I realized THIS was really the beginning of the Transcontinental Race I had been so eagerly looking forward to for many weeks.

She explained that the plane was a stock model, nothing "souped up" nor filled with special equipment. Nevertheless, she felt this was the best plane she'd ever flown. Two days later, she received flight instructions ordering the pilots to fly to the Palm Springs starting point that afternoon to avoid heavy weather. They took off at 5:50 p.m. to join the other planes already waiting in Palm Springs for the

Frannie in Ryan Navion's brand new plane

race to begin at dawn the next day. Through heavy rain, low ceiling, and poor visibility, Frannie made three attempts at different altitudes before she made it in, "partly between layers and then over the top." She was relieved to have her feet on the ground at Palm Springs.

> Up at 3:00 AM, no one got more than about an hour's sleep, ready for takeoff at dawn. One contestant withdrew her Bonanza after seeing a Ryan Navion was in the race, leaving six to duke it out. Three Cessnas, a Stinson, a Bellanca Cruisair, and a Ryan Navion.

Having drawn lots for takeoff at five-minute intervals, Frannie was second. She noted that one Cessna was piloted by twins: One held the women's altitude record for soaring, and the other was a weather expert. They seemed like an unbeatable duo. Each plane carried a time handicap based on the manufacturer's estimated cruising speed. The sponsors of the Bellanca told Frannie that the pilot was going to fly full throttle all the way, leaving Frannie worried about her new engine's performance.

As they set off, they were flying a straight line to Tuscon but into headwinds of 40 mph, unusual for flights heading east. When she reached the Tuscon area:

> Tuscon radio reported severe thunderstorms in the El Paso area, which, coupled with headwinds, would have allowed me too little margin of gasoline to weave around storms, or to return to another airport. I whipped into a small field a few miles ahead, gassed the airplane, and was off in eight minutes. The headwinds continued and so did the reports of thunderstorms. I began to see them a hundred miles west of El Paso. It looked like great columns of rain pouring out of a boiling mass of cumulonimbus clouds. Zigzag stripes of lightening appeared, so bright that it almost took my breath away. But the storms were scattered

Pilots readying for competition. Frannie (third from the right) leans in to discuss the route. The twin pilots look on from the back row.

> enough [for me] to bypass them, and I approached El Paso from the south while a great blackness hovered over the west of the city.

Frannie landed safely to learn that the next pass was closed. "The pilots decided to take off the next morning and get some sleep."

Up again at 3:00 a.m., and on the runway at dawn, Frannie didn't see the other pilots again until they met in Miami. She flew above the next mountain pass by climbing to 14,000 feet over broken clouds, but she still faced headwinds. Then she noticed:

> The engine wasn't purring quite so smoothly. The carburetor heat and mixture control didn't help any. No, it wasn't my imagination — a magneto check gave me a thrill — the left one was completely out! I was chugging along nicely on the right one, and although breaks began to appear in the clouds beneath me, I decided to stay with my flight plan, which took me to Waco, Texas. Over San Angelo, the clouds became scattered, and soon after that the sky was clear. I stayed up there at 14,000 until I could see Waco, then started a slow let-down that would still give me plenty of gliding range if the right magneto got too tired. At four minutes past nine, I taxied up to the Waco Aviation School hanger, where the chief mechanic and two others went to work at once on that magneto.

An airplane's magneto is an engine-driven generator that uses magnets and coils to ignite spark plugs to fire the engine. Planes have two, so if one fails, the engine continues to run, but less efficiently.

Frannie continued to explain that the mechanics wouldn't allow her to pay for the long, difficult repairs. After trying to fix the faulty part, the mechanics had to fly to Dallas to pick up a new magneto and coil. Disheartened by having to wait for so long in beautiful weather, Frannie

> . . . decided to find a hairdressing salon and make an attempt to repair the effects of the preceding day's wind and rain. While in that most unattractive of all spots — under the hair dryer — two gentlemen appeared, one carrying a large camera and flash bulbs. They were pointing in my direction,

and presently came over and told me they were from the Waco press. They had heard I was in the All-Women's Transcontinental Air Race and thought it would be a novel angle to get a picture of me under the dryer. You may well imagine my horror at such an idea, and I gently but firmly persuaded them that a picture with the airplane would have much greater appeal.

By that evening, C-4304K was ready to go. With true Texas hospitality, Floyd Gray, president of Waco Aviation, had coffee with me at 4:00 AM, drove me to the airport, pushed the airplane out of the hangar, checked the weather, and waved me good luck as I taxied out. One stop between there and Miami would do it, and a crosswind landing at Pensacola brought me close to the gas pit, saving several precious minutes. I was out of there in practically no time, and up to 15,000 [feet] I went, where at long last I had a good tail boost. A whiff of oxygen at intervals from my tiny portable oxygen bottle kept me 'awake and aware,' and at that altitude I felt perfectly safe in cutting a corner of the Gulf over Cross City, then direct to a point just east of Palm Beach, where I started the let-down which clocked me over the east-west runway of Amelia Earhart Field in Miami at 14:22 EST. [Cumulative] time for the entire trip was 17:10, which despite headwinds that prevailed throughout the first part of the trip, gave me an average of 150 mph, the exact speed at which I was handicapped.

'Mother' Earhart, who is dearly loved by all of us 99ers, greeted me at the field, and it was a real pleasure to see her there again this year.

Although I was awfully glad to be there myself, I was almost sorry the race was all over for me, because it had been so much fun.

Mother of 7 Lands Derby Racer Here

Mrs. Frances Nolde of Reading, Pa., mother of seven children, is shown above leaving the Ryan Navion plane she is piloting in the Transcontinental Air Derby for Women. She landed at the Municipal Airport here because of magneto trouble. She will continue her flight to Miami Thursday morning.

Powder Puff Derby Flyer, Mother of Seven, Stops In Waco for Motor Checkover

Back from the hairdresser

• DARLING OF THE PRESS •

The newspaper articles that followed Frannie's race added detail to her journal. The *Waco News-Tribune* showed a picture of her not under a hair dryer but newly coiffed and standing on the wing of her plane, with the heading, "Powder Puff Derby Flyer, Mother of Seven, Stops in Waco for Motor Checkover." The article says, "She's a blonde-haired Dutch lassie from Reading, Pa., just five feet, five inches tall, weighing in at 112 pounds and the mother of seven children, but she hurtled her Ryan Navion plane from Palm Springs, Calif. to Waco in nine hours and 30 minutes." They describe the magneto problem and then explain why she won: "Her seven children, four of them 'inherited' when she married Hans W. Nolde, are one of the reasons she had been leading the race up until the time she landed here. 'I must hurry to Miami and then on to Reading by Monday so I can do the laundry for the youngsters,' she said."

During the race, Frannie carried U.S. mail bearing the Amelia Earhart memorial stamp, which collectors purchased to raise money for the Amelia Earhart Memorial Foundation for Women Pilots.

With the race over, Earhart's mother emerged to welcome Frannie to Amelia Earhart Field. Frannie, on bended knee on the wing of her plane, reached out to shake hands with Mrs. Amy Otis Earhart. By then, Frannie knew she had won the race.

In a delightful irony for those who knew Frannie well, she was then congratulated by her rival, Jackie Cochran, the sponsor of the race who had put up $1,500 in prize money, and for winning, Mother won $500 (about $5,000 today).

• MOTHER AND JACKIE •

Although Mother once held the American woman solo-hour record, other female pilots soon caught up. In Frannie's eyes, her main rival was Jackie Cochran. According to

"Mother" Earhart greets Frannie; official timekeeper looks on.

Superwoman Jacqueline Cochran, family memories written by her niece, not only was Jackie a skilled pilot but her appearance was also stunning. And after she married a multi-millionaire, she seemed to achieve everything a female pilot could hope for. Eventually, Jackie overshadowed even Amelia Earhart, the best-known female pilot of the 1930s, who became a legend when her plane disappeared over the Pacific in 1937.

Jackie Cochran held over 200 speed, altitude, and distance records, more than any other pilot of her time, male or female. One of few women to win the Bendix Air Race for high-performance planes, she held a leading role in the Women Airforce Service Pilots (WASPS) during WWII and participated in the NASA space program.

The two women differed, however, in their interest in helping propel girls and young women into aviation roles. Jackie's biographer says Jackie had a "surprising reluctance to crusade for the advancement of women." She railed against female liberation and became enmeshed in a controversy about women's place in the military. She didn't advocate spending money to train female pilots, saying they might marry, get pregnant, and drop out. By contrast, Frannie always promoted the training of CAP girl cadets and women to take leadership roles in aviation, besting Jackie as an early feminist.

AP Wirephoto

CHAMP GREETS CHAMP—Eight years after she decided to beat her fear of planes, Mrs. Frances Nolde (left) won the 2600 mile cross-country race from California to Miami. Here, she receives congratulations from veteran pilot Jacqueline Cochran, sponsor of the event.

Frannie thrilled to win

Seeing Jackie as her nemesis, Frannie had to protect herself with a confident edge that concealed frustration, disappointment, and hurt which began to show later in life.

She ends her Powder Puff Derby journal by writing:

> Jacqueline Cochran provided the big drama on Saturday, when she flew in from Washington in her Lockheed Lodestar, taxied to the ramp, stepped out immaculate in a lovely white sharkskin dress, and gaily unfurled a red taffeta parasol as she strolled casually away from that great flying machine! Incidentally, it was she who sponsored the Transcontinental Air Race, awarding the prize money as well as the really handsome trophy. It will remain my most cherished possession for all time.

Posing with her trophy in front of a Jonas Lei painting

One newspaper wrote,

Berks 'Sky Queen' Due Home today.

> Mrs. Frances Nolde, of Sheerlund, winner of the 2,600-mile women's pilot transcontinental air race from California-to-Miami, Fla., is expected to arrive home 'sometime today,' a member of the Nolde household said last night.
>
> The exact time is not known, but it was said she may arrive this afternoon, piloting the Navion which she flew across the country to win the first-place prize.

A reporter described her arrival home: "Mrs. Nolde's husband, chairman of the board of directors of the Nolde & Horst Company, received the news of his wife's victory while confined to bed at his home in Sheerlund. He is convalescing with a fractured back sustained in a fall at his home several weeks ago."

• DADDY'S FLIGHT •

On occasion, Daddy walked in his sleep. One night, a few weeks before the Powder Puff Derby, he got out of bed, still asleep, walked through the bathroom and dressing room, opened the window, climbed onto the radiator, and walked out the window. He fell from the second story, landed on his feet, then toppled over, having broken his back. He crawled through the open porch to reach the heavy wooden door with its iron swing-loop handle. Somehow, he reached up, opened the door, and crawled into the living room. From there, he called Mother for help.

Daddy's Window

Waking up in the bedroom above the living room, she barely heard his faint call from downstairs. She jumped out of bed, grabbed her nightgown and negligee, rushed down the hall, and descended the circular staircase to find Daddy halfway under a chair. She phoned for help and rushed back upstairs to get dressed and await the ambulance ride to the hospital.

With Daddy injured, and the Derby fast approaching, they debated what to do. Though Mother had misgivings, Daddy would not stop her from flying in the race. They hired a full-time nurse, Miss Phlum, known as "Phlumie," to come daily. That solved the problem.

When Mother arrived home with her tall trophy in hand, she placed it next to Daddy's hospital bed. He was recuperating in the living room, not far from where mother had found him after his fall.

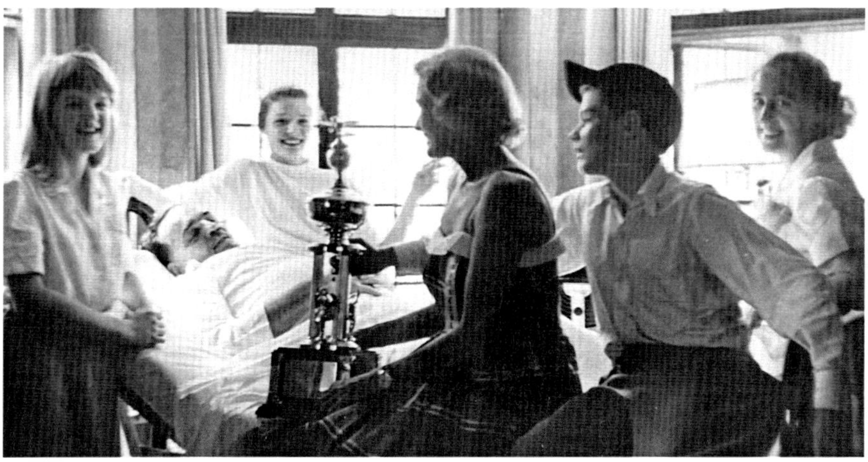

Celebrating her trophy: from left, Francie, Daddy, Sally, Mother, Chris, and Daddy's nurse, Miss Phlum

Daddy seemed genuinely proud that Mother received national attention. He ended a letter to Jeanne in August of 1948, "Mother is of course still flying all over the lot and since she won that Powder Puff Transcontinental race, she is pretty cocky. Since she put the big, beautiful trophy which she won in the living room, I collected all my tennis trophies and put them up in the attic. The comparison was terrible."

• PUBLIC ACCLAIM •

A year later, Frannie entered the international race from Montreal to Miami. Given a handicap for her Ryan Navion, she came in third, with her close friend Vi Delp as co-pilot. That was the end of her racing career. She was made contest chair for the next racing cycle, and contest chairs weren't allowed to race.

Frannie sponsored a follow-up race herself; one newspaper reported, "Miss Kay Menges of Hackensack, N.J. was announced as the winner of the New York-to-Miami Derby sponsored by Mrs. Nolde. Miss Menges will receive $250 first prize money."

Because the airplane Frannie raced in 1948 did not belong to her, it wasn't long before Hans bought her *Reposa IV*, her first, very own, Navion. She was thrilled. Hans replaced Frannie's Navions with updated versions, the last named *Reposa VII*. "Reposa" is a Spanish word meaning "rest." She was in total repose when flying alone.

Frannie's love of solo flying, her war efforts, and her competitive success brought her national aviation responsibilities.

CHAPTER THIRTEEN

"The Colonel is a Lady"

• WAR ENDS, FRANNIE CONTINUES •

By the end of the war, Frannie had been promoted from second lieutenant to first lieutenant to captain and finally, in 1951, to full colonel as head of the CAP national women's program. The family knew she should have become a general, but we weren't familiar with the word "misogyny," and in those days women never became generals. Nevertheless, we called Mother "General," saluting her whenever she appeared in uniform.

Reflecting concerns Hans had expressed years before, *The Philadelphia Inquirer Magazine* explained that Frannie had not slowed down. The article's headline reads, "The Colonel Is a Lady. She's Training 30,000 Girl Civil Air Patrol Cadets and Still Finds Time to Rear a Family of Seven." The article begins:

> No official record is available for confirmation, but friends of Hans W. Nolde maintain that he is the only person in the United States who has his breakfast prepared by a colonel. His wife is Frances W. Nolde, recently commissioned a colonel in the Civil Air Patrol — the only woman in the history of the CAP to hold so high a rank.
>
> Like many another housewife, the colonel rises early each day at Sheerlund, the Nolde's 22-room home on

Mrs. Frances W. Nolde, the only woman colonel in the Civil Air Patrol, has seven children, didn't take up flying until she was 39.

The Colonel Is a Lady

She's Training 30,000 Girl Civil Air Patrol Cadets

And Still Finds Time to Rear a Family of Seven

> the outskirts of Reading, Pa., and serves breakfast to her husband. Then Nolde, a hosiery manufacturer, goes to his office, and Colonel Nolde goes off into the wild blue yonder.
>
> "I enjoy cooking," she says, "It is exciting to turn out good meals — almost as exciting as flying."

Mother's comment reflects the pressure on her to play the expected role of homemaker and mother of seven while pursuing a career in aviation. The pre-feminist culture pushed her to lie; she was not preparing meals at home, and flying remained her overriding passion. Moreover, when the article was written, only two children remained at Punches Run; Chris and I were at boarding school, home only in the summer. At the same time, Mother and Daddy's arguments became more heated.

By 1951, Mother was spending more and more time in her Washington office, and her marriage relationship was strained. While Mother was publicly revered and touted as an extraordinary woman, privately she certainly was hurt, knowing by then that her husband was interested in someone else.

• LIFE AS A FEMALE COLONEL •

War had been a masculine endeavor until women took leadership roles in the WWII American effort and changed some of the dynamics. In 1944, Frannie started training young female and male cadets, persuading Sally and Jake to join one summer, proud to have young family members participate. With the war over, her efforts broadened when she became commander in 1951 of the women's program for the CAP.

The Philadelphia Inquirer reported:

> Colonel Nolde, whose primary job is supervising … girl cadets between the ages of 15 and 18, is no armchair flier. Now 49, and mother of seven, she has been flying since 1941.
>
> "That [CAP] experience," she says, "convinced me that women can play a vital role in aviation, especially during times of national emergency, by replacing pilots who have gone into the service. That's why it's important that, in the present emergency, girls participate in the CAP cadet training program and help the nation prepare for any crisis that might eventuate."
>
> From her office in Washington, Colonel Nolde, adviser to General Lucas V. Beau, national commander of the Civil Air Patrol, … keeps an eye on the girl cadet training program in the 52 wings of CAP. The training program is designed to teach the girls the rudiments of navigation, meteorology and communications, familiarize them with instruments and give them basic training in working with aircraft mechanisms. The aim is to teach the girls everything but actual flying.
>
> Col. Nolde … is recommending Girl Scout leaders organize wing scouts to take advantage of aviation classes. Such training not only develops self-confidence and character but it prepares girls for many jobs open to them in fields of aviation. Some of them will no doubt go on to take flying lessons, preparing themselves for service to their country in case of emergency.

In 1952, the *CAP Recruiting Journal* reported:

> Most prominent among women in Civil Air Patrol today is Col. Frances W. Nolde of Reading, PA, who heads the women's program. A veteran of nearly 10 years in CAP, Colonel Nolde has a multitude of aeronautical interests in

Frannie teaches female CAP cadets

city, state, and national aviation circles. Wherever aviators meet, the junketing flier is likely to meet Colonel Nolde and her crimson Ryan Navion — the lady's sixth airplane in some 4500 hours of flying.

All through the ranks of women in Civil Air Patrol are to be found the girls who may one day skipper the better jobs for American Aviation ... for, as volunteers in their CAP work, these women have demonstrated their ability to compete in any class.

• WOMEN'S VOICES •

Frannie had stepped into a world surrounded by men, and she responded to that male-dominated world by voicing and expressing women's abilities to contribute and lead. Having Chris and me at boarding school made it possible for her to travel and take leadership roles.

In the early '50s, Frannie was the "Ranking CAP Woman Officer" to attend a four-day dedication of the new Broome County Airport on Mt. Ettrick in Binghamton, New York. The local headline reads, "Big Brass to Play Key Dedication Roles; Ranking CAP Woman Officer Included." By then, the CAP had 75,000 members, including 15,000 women, many of whom flew their own planes.

As she became busier and busier with the CAP, Mother was home less often, more engaged with flying than anything else at a time when Daddy was hanging on to his business by his fingernails.

A woman's voice

es Stop Reds

General Joins Armed Forces Day Group at Luncheon

Military leaders at the Armed Forces Day luncheon at noon today in the Abraham Lincoln Hotel are pictured here. Left to right they are: Col. Frances Nolde, of the Civil Air Patrol; Commander A. W. Dimwiddie, area project officer; Maj. Gen. Laurence B. Keiser, commander of Indiantown Gap Military Reservation, and Col. L. Lee Bittenbender, chairman of the Armed Forces' Day committee.

(Eagle Staff Photo.)

WOMEN IN AVIATION is a topic dear to the heart of Mrs. Frances Nolde, consultant to the Defense Air Transportation Administration. In 1951 she was appointed adviser on women's activities to the national commander of the Civil Air Patrol, Maj. Gen. Lucas V. Beau.

With CAP General Beau, a good friend.

• HONORING THE CIVIL AIR PATROL •

In 2014, President Obama awarded the Civil Air Patrol the Distinguished Gold Medal of Honor for its wartime years, 1941-1945. He signed legislation awarding approximately 200,000 World War II members of CAP the country's highest expression of appreciation for distinguished achievements and contributions.

On December 10, Chris and I watched Speaker of the House John Boehner present the medal to CAP National Commander Major General Joseph R. Vazquez and former U.S. Representative Lester L. Wolff, himself a wartime member of the New York Wing.

Both sides of the Congressional Medal

One side of the medal depicts a Stinson Voyager 10A aircraft, armed with demolition bombs, escorting an oil tanker. The aircraft has the CAP coastal patrol roundel and the number 65, representing the number of CAP members killed during the war. Two civilian volunteers, a male coastal patrol observer and a female pilot, search the sky for enemy planes. The other side honors civilian volunteers for their unusual contributions in World War II.

Decades after Mother's energetic work in WWII, Chris and I were deeply moved as CAP officials read her name and a summary of her contributions. The dramatic ceremony included a video of single-engine planes, with bombs strapped to their underbellies, dive-bombing a German submarine. We also viewed the faces of 65 CAP pilots who did not survive the war. We brought home replicas of the medal as a way for family members to remember Mother.

A CAP aircraft pulls out after a near miss of a German U-Boat.

CHAPTER FOURTEEN

Postwar Flying

• SIME AND BRIGHTY •

Before the war, Frannie's friends Alfred "Sime" Bertolet and Robert "Brighty" Brighthaupt bought Reading Aviation Service (RAS). A sales and maintenance operation for light aircraft, RAS made Reading Airport accessible to both commercial and private airplanes.

After Pearl Harbor, they signed a U.S. Army contract for military pilot training. During the war, they wanted to leave RAS to join the Army Air Corps, but the government contract almost stopped Sime; he was expected to stay to manage the pilot training obligation. Arguing others could fulfill that part of the RAS contract, he squeaked out of it. Sime and Brighty both succeeded in becoming Army pilots, returning home safely after the war.

As a director, Frannie helped reestablish RAS, giving financial support to the privately owned operation. RAS provided aircraft fueling, hangar space, tie-down, parking, rental, maintenance, flight instruction, and other essential services.

As kids, we loved Sime's energetic expression, beaming smile, and warm hug. Sime gave of himself totally when he visited our home; we responded with our affection. We also adored Brighty for his delicious sense of humor and original jokes. These men were bright spots in our lives.

During the war, Sime flew the "Hump" in the China, Burma, India Theater of Operations. At the end of the war, he brought home Magda, a beautiful, French-speaking woman from Casablanca, to be his "war bride." Magda came to the United States with great courage, her signature quality. And Frannie took Magda under her wing. Despite their age difference, the two women became fast friends. During a family reunion in Reading in the early 1980s, Magda repeatedly mentioned Mother's kindness in helping a young bride feel welcomed in America.

• THE READING AIR SHOW: BEST IN THE NATION •

A few years before WWII, Reading conducted air shows as trade shows, operated by the airport authority. When the Army expanded the airport in 1941 to six times larger, military operations replaced air shows. At the end of the war, the Reading flying community, its flying clubs, and RAS created a modest air show. It wasn't until 1949, however, that RAS created a full-blown air show to promote and package their products. RAS took charge and engaged Frannie as director of the air show for the next few years. She catapulted Reading into the public limelight: the Reading Air Show was called "the best in the Nation, second only to the Paris Air Show." What started as a trade show had become topnotch entertainment.

With Frannie's vision and creativity, the air show offered something for everyone: precision formation flying, drops of clustered parachutists, war planes exhibited on the ground and in the air, biplanes, precision aerobatics, and daring pilots performing unique tricks. Vintage WWII planes flew overhead. Pilots in smaller planes performed loops, rolls, and low-altitude maneuvers; they spilled smoke trails from the tails and wings of their planes, keeping viewers spellbound, on the edge of their seats and cheering for more.

Chris and I thought the most exciting part of Mother's aviation career was the Reading Air Show. We loved the airplanes flying in formation, the aerobatic stunts, and the many parachutists dropping at once and "spilling wind."

Giving Private Flying a Boost

The Reading Aviation Association got off to a flying postwar start last night when more than 200 persons attended a clambake and dance at the Reading Municipal Airport. More than 25 planes, most of them owned by association members, were on display.

WWII Vought FU4 Corsair fighter plane

Showing off varieties of war planes

Parachute cluster

Show planes in formation

• BEVO HOWARD •

Mother invited one or two outstanding aerobatic pilots to be part of the program each year. Pilots like Beverly "Bevo" Howard performed breathtaking stunts. No one could match Bevo.

Bevo's life illustrated the success of a person who grabbed every opportunity. Like Mother, he had "the disease," an addiction to flying. Flamboyant and charismatic showmanship belied his pride of being a conservative businessman. His 15-minute performance of 40 maneuvers, finishing with an extraordinary stunt of flying upside down, captured the hearts and minds of spectators.

Higher education had nothing to offer him compared to his ambition to fly, so he dropped out of junior college at the age of 18

Bevo, "Look Ma, no hands!"

Bevo and his Piper Cub

to join Hawthorne Aviation in Charleston, South Carolina. At the age of 21, he bought the failing Hawthorne and turned it into a multimillion-dollar operation. Also, at the age of 21, he became the youngest commercial airline copilot for Eastern Airlines.

Some apocryphal stories about Bevo's life make him sound like a childhood genius and entrepreneur, asserting he went to work for Hawthorne Aviation when 14, bought it a few years later, learned to fly by the age of 16, became the youngest transport pilot for Delta and Eastern at age 18, and flew both right and left seat on DC-10s. I'd love to believe some of that was true.

Bevo started flying in airshows in 1933, and by 1938, he was known for being the first pilot to fly an outside loop in a light plane — a 37 ½ horsepower Piper Cub. His most famous maneuver was an "inverted ribbon pickup," in which he'd fly a bi-plane upside down and grab a red ribbon held by someone on the ground but more often held between two poles. It was both terrifying and thrilling. I wondered if I'd ever have the courage to stand there holding a red ribbon with Bevo's plane heading straight for me, upside down and seven feet off the ground.

Bevo always stayed at our house during the few days of the Reading Show. Giving us time and attention, Bevo quickly became our favorite aerobatic pilot. He performed the aerobatic tricks we wished Mother would do.

Only later did we learn how much Bevo gave of himself to others, particularly to those new to aerobatic flying. He was known for sharing his experience, knowledge, and heart. Like us, many flyers respected and loved Bevo. After we left Reading, we didn't see him again. But we learned of his tragic death in 1971. While flying his Bucker Bu 133 Jungmeister at an air show in Greenville, North Carolina, his engine reportedly failed, and he clipped a tree, knocking off a wing and plunging to the ground. We felt the horror, grief, and dismay for a long time.

• HOMETOWN SHOWS AND NAMING AIRPORTS •

Before leaving Reading in 1953, Frannie was involved in the re-naming of two airports: one after herself, the other after General Carl. A. Spaatz.

In Frannie's hometown, Deposit, New York, the 1950 Air Show program honored those involved in the incorporation of the Deposit Airport and Frannie's role in the air show. By then, her devotion to the field of aviation and those involved with flying eclipsed her ambivalent feelings about Deposit, a place associated with her father. She was able to offer her expertise and financial resources to the town's effort to promote aviation. What mixed feelings she might have felt, she didn't exhibit.

The program states the following:

> Late in the fall of 1949 an addition was built on the hanger. Soon after that, plans were made for a 1950 airshow.
>
> A very important person in making the air show a reality was Frances Wilcox Nolde. [In] the January DHS newsletter article on the air show, she had guaranteed to foot the bill for any losses incurred by the air show.

Frances Wilcox Nolde

To whom we gratefully dedicate the 1950 Deposit Air Show.

Frances Wilcox Nolde, now of Reading, Pennsylvania, still has a warm spot for her hometown, Deposit, New York. To the "Old Timers" at Deposit, Mrs. Nolde is remembered as one of the beautiful daughters of Fred Wilcox, who was known far and wide as a dealer and owner of horses, a sportsman, and to the writer's own memory, one of the nicest and most gentlemanly of men in Deposit.

When Frances Nolde becomes interested in something, that something immediately gets a boost, and a continuous one. She started flying in 1941 — and has no intention of stopping. Her first plane was a Piper Cub. In 1942 she obtained a commercial pilot's license and a new coupe. Later she owned a Fairchild 24 and since then, the Navions.

During the war years she was "Line Dispatcher" for the Cadet Training Program under War Training Service. She operated the Courier Service at Reading, Pennsylvania, for the Civil Air Patrol in which she held the rank of Captain. In the meantime, she flew cargo and war industry personnel.

Francie and Chris with Mother at her airport dedication

In 1951, Deposit dedicated its new airport to Mother, calling it *The Frances Wilcox Nolde Airport.* Mother, Chris, and I flew up for the ceremony, without Daddy. In keeping with her ambivalent feelings, Mother did not show us where she grew up or any place associated with her father's family.

At the end of Mother's acceptance speech, she invited the whole town of Deposit to attend the Reading Air Show she had been planning for months. One person from Deposit took her invitation personally. As an adult, I wrote about it in my recollections of life at Punches Run:

Early-Bird Spectator

In 1951, Mother flew Chris and me to her birthplace, Deposit, New York, to participate in the dedication of their new airport in her name. During her speech, she invited everybody to attend the Reading Air Show in two weeks. After all, she was running the air show and knew all the flyers and acrobatic pilots.

Two mornings later, at 5:00 AM, my parents heard someone driving up the long, gravel driveway. In the summertime, with our windows open, we could hear cars long before they reached the house. However, this one stopped short of the front circle. A door opened. Someone got out. The door slammed shut. The car turned around and headed back down the hill. Footsteps crunched on the stone driveway.

Daddy bolted out of bed and grabbed his revolver. He came down the hall, passed my bedroom, and continued on to waken Jake. I could hear tones but not specific words. I lay in bed frozen with fear.

Daddy and Jake went down the back stairs and out the side door. Finding nothing amiss, they came inside, talked between themselves, then went back out and headed for the three-car garage. Through the open doors, they saw a strange man sitting quietly in the yellow Jeep.

Daddy gripped the revolver in his pocket. Something told him not to bring it out. Daddy approached the strange man and asked, "Who are you? What are you doing here?"

The man told him Mrs. Nolde had spoken at the Deposit Air Show and invited him to the Reading Air Show. He had bought a round-trip bus ticket with his savings. When he arrived in the city early in the morning, he asked about the air show and was told it was two weeks away. He stated he wanted to see Mrs. Frances

Nolde because she had invited him to come. A taxi driver, knowing how to find Punches Run, had driven him out to The Place and dropped him off.

Daddy explained the misunderstanding, called another taxi to collect the man, paid the fare, and sent him back home. Later, Mother learned he was a well-known and troubled man.

The circle

• RENAMING THE READING AIRPORT •

In 1949, Frannie became the first woman to sit on the Reading Airport Commission, and from that vantage point, she worked to have the airport named for Pennsylvanian "Tooey" Spaatz, retired chief of staff of the U.S. Air Force. She worked closely with Reading Municipal Airport Secretary-Manager Melvin H. Nuss, a hardworking friend, to make it happen. On August 12, 1951, the Reading Municipal Airport was dedicated *The General Carl. A. Spaatz Field.*

The U.S. Air Force website includes a biography of Carl Andrew "Tooey" Spaatz. A graduate of the U.S. Military Academy, General Spaatz became the first chief of staff of the U.S. Air Force in 1947,

Frannie hanging out with General Spaatz (center) and "the guys"

appointed by President Truman. He directly contributed to the defeat of Germany by successfully pressing for bombing of their oil production facilities rather than other targets. He was interred at the U.S. Air Force Academy in 1974. Mother considered him a good friend.

The Mid-Atlantic Air Museum at Spaatz Field collects and restores historic planes and classic airliners as well as rare civilian and military aircraft. The museum has welcomed not only "warbirds" but also two Navions from the mid-'40s. Planes that flew in Frannie's shows and planes she flew herself have become museum pieces.

For many years, those wonderful planes had been part of Frannie's fame as a newsworthy heroine.

Placing a portrait of General Spaatz at the airport

PART FIVE

Heroine

CHAPTER FIFTEEN
Myths and Family Stories

• NEWSWORTHY MOTHER •

At the start of Frannie's flying career, reporters mixed facts with fiction when writing about this beautiful pilot-mother, creating a larger-than-life persona.

As news organizations began to capture Frannie's active aviator's life with stories and glamorous photographs, "housekeeping" became a glorifying myth. A cook and a full-time couple lived in the "Servants' Quarters." Once a week, a laundress washed clothes, and a helper ironed sheets, shirts, and table linen. Amused, Frannie basked in the myth about her housekeeping.

Portraying her in action, either in her plane or shaking hands with dignitaries, reporters said she wasn't a "petticoat pilot," but was "beautifully groomed." They said she had 110 hats and bought one more because she thought it was "so pretty." Photographs often showed her carrying a purse AND a hat box.

While most newspapers focused on her beauty, some articles took a more serious vein. *The Binghamton Sun* commented, "The art of flying, she has since concluded, is one of those basic skills which everyone should know. It is not as tough on an old learner with the airplane as with the automobile, she feels. There is no traffic problem 'up there.' Frannie claimed, 'I'll keep on flying until I'm so old I can't crawl out of a wheelchair! ... The art of flying will become one of those basic skills that everyone should know.'"

EVENING TRIBUNE SAN DIEGO, CALIFORNIA WEDNESDAY, APRIL 15, 1959

Blonde Flier Confers Here

Woman Acts as Liaison For Aviation Group

By BETTY PEACH

A slender blonde woman with 110 hats and seven children was in San Diego this week to confer with local committee heads on the International Civil Aviation Organization Conference, which opens June 16 in Balboa Park.

She is Mrs. Frances Wilcox Nolde, of Washington, D.C., a veteran flier with some 5,000 hours on her log book. Her official job is director of the General Aviation Division of the Defense Air Transportation Administration of the Department of Commerce.

Here, and during the international conference, she is serving as the liaison official for the president's Air Coordinating Committee.

Holds Local Talks

She conferred locally with John D. Butler, general chairman of the civic committee for the conference, which is expected to attract more than 1,000 civil aviation leaders from 73 nations; with Gerald Crary of the Convention and Tourist Bureau, and Mrs. John S. Lockwood of the San Diego chapter of Ninety-Nines, who will arrange activities for the wives who will attend the conference.

Highly enthusiastic about her work, Mrs. Nolde is equally enthusiastic about the choice of San Diego for the convention.

"I had never been on the ground here, although I have flown over San Diego, and have many friends here through the Ninety-Nines to which I belong.

Learns in 1940

"When they asked me in Washington to take the job, I phoned Betty Gillies (local flier and Ninety-Nines member) and asked for help. She suggested Gertrude Lockwood, and we were on our way to getting the thing organized," she said.

Mrs. Nolde learned to fly in 1940.

"Principally," she said with an impish grin, "to get away from my seven small children. I would fly off in an

nese and teaches Far East economy. Another son teaches in a boys' school in Connecticut, and the other son is in college and is going to Switzerland to work this summer.

Girls Are Married

"All four girls are married. One lives in Palo Alto, one in New York, one in England, and one in Bakersfield. She leaves next month with her husband for Nigeria. There are eight grandchildren."

Mrs. Nolde now lives alone in a house in Georgetown, only a 10-minute drive to the office, where she has worked six years.

"Ours is the smallest agency in the government—there are four of us, and two secretaries," she said.

Many Wives Expected

"It is quite a plum for San Diego to get this conference," Mrs. Nolde explained. "Seattle wanted it very much. This is the first time the conference has been held in the United States since the founding of the International Civil Aviation Organization in 1944, when the conference was held in Chicago.

"This is the 12th such meeting. The last one, in Caracas, Venezuela, drew a big attendance, with about 100 women attending with their husbands. We figure this year since it is in the United States, it will attract many more wives, and we do want to have an interesting program arranged for them.

Buys New Hat

"That certainly will be easy to do, with such fascinating things to see here. The climate alone will be heavenly.

MRS. FRANCES WILCOX NOLDE
That box is full of hats, too.

The ubiquitous hat box

Her collection of yellowed newspaper clippings chronicle much of her aviator's life, reporters making small errors but not straying far from the truth. Stories of her successes in aviation followed a consistent theme: a mother of seven children became a pilot in a man's world. There she introduced young women to a world of aviation where, through science and communications, they could excel and find equal opportunities for themselves. A time of patriarchal culture often suppressed women's aptitude and skill by praising only their beauty, not their abilities. She demonstrated that a woman could be as good a pilot as any man.

An *Oregon Journal* article said, "Flying 16,000 miles over seven Western states, to Alaska and Hawaii, is a lot easier than nursing three babies down with whooping cough at one time. Being a courier air base commander for Civil Air Patrol (Reading, Pa.), directing both men and women fliers in jobs that expedited World War II, took less diplomacy than keeping the peace at the dining table between three sets of children.

"Frances welded them into a happy family, with the aid of child psychology she'd taken at Syracuse University. Now the youngest is 14, and with the approval of her husband, Frances is free to fly again."

The chauvinistic comment about getting permission from her husband to fly was nonsense. Frannie did not need Hans' permission to fly. Hans had encouraged and supported her interest from the very beginning, and he continued to do so until he realized that Frannie found her flying more important than her marriage.

• DADDY'S SHIRTS •

Two newspapers quoted Mother as saying she had to rush home from winning the Powder Puff Derby to do laundry for the children. That was nonsense, too.

One spring vacation, I asked if we could go to church on Easter morning. We never went to church, but schoolmates talked about their religions, and I was fascinated. Mother said we couldn't go because she had to iron Daddy's shirts, even though I knew she never did. In response, I quietly got up at 5:00 in the morning, found Daddy's shirts in the ironing basket, and began to iron them. I created scorches and creases, but I did the best a little girl could. When Mother woke up, I told her we could go to church because I had ironed all Daddy's shirts. Mother quietly relented by driving Chris and me into the city, leaving us at some cathedral-like building, and telling us she'd be back to pick us up in an hour.

• KILLER ON THE LOOSE •

Mother's fame, influence, and even notoriety carried inherent dangers. When Sally entered Bennington College at 18, and then married her 35-year-old freshman English teacher, Chris and I were the only children still at home during summer vacations. One night, I suddenly woke up to sounds of rustling and rattling. Looking down the hallway reflected in my closet mirror, I could see Mother standing in the doorway of her room, back lit, holding THE revolver by her side. Daddy was traveling for business. She seemed to be listening for something. Pulling up my covers, I froze. The phone rang, and Mother disappeared, leaving only her shadow in the doorway. Between fits of sleep, I watched her bedroom light and heard murmurings of phone calls.

For the rest of the night, I heard creaking sounds and imagined someone creeping up the back stairs which opened onto a hallway where Chris and I slept. I was sure an intruder would come into my bedroom first, so I tried to stay awake all night but dozed off and on. When I woke to early morning light, I felt confident enough to run down the hallway to Mother's room. She told me a story which became part of family lore.

Sally's husband, from whom she was separated, had called Sally to tell her he was driving to Punches Run to kill Mother for encouraging

Sally to leave him. When Mother received Sally's warning, she alerted the State Police to watch for the professor's license plate on the highways. She then called Daddy, grabbed the revolver, and drummed up her courage for a confrontation, alone.

I was relieved it had been a false alarm, but my young nerves were jangled for a long time. I continued to hear creaking noises on the back stairway until I believed we were free from a death threat by a menacing man. After Daddy made new keys for the many unusual locks in the eight doors that made us vulnerable, we lost that glorious feeling of being free by living out in the country with unlocked doors. In the end, however, not even Mother and Daddy locked our doors. Too much trouble.

• MYSTERIOUS GIFTS •

When some of Mother's friends died, they designated Mother the beneficiary of many unusual items. On my visits to Washington, I'd see an accumulation of new things: oriental rugs, a Quan Yin rose quartz lamp, monogramed silverware, assorted pieces of decorative china, and elaborate flower vases, all unfamiliar to life at Punches Run.

One donor of the oriental rugs and silverware was probably Admiral Emory Scott Land, Mother's dear friend and a man 23 years her senior. As a widower, he visited Mother often. I thought he was Edwin Land, the developer of Polaroid and the Land Camera. How wrong could I be?

He was a superb navel ship inventor of submarines, Liberty Ships, Victory Ships, and merchant ships during WWII.

Sumptuous gift:
Quan Yin rose quartz lamp

Time cover, Admiral Land

During one of his visits when Chris and I were feeling mischievous, we presented Admiral Land with a dessert of ice cream with candied fruit sprinkled on top. We enjoyed watching the poor soul try to chew rock-hard nuggets that were so dried out they were impossible to soften. He worked on it and worked on it, but the fruit kept getting stuck in his teeth. We hoped he'd stop coming around.

• ROBBERS OF JEWELRY •

One day, I noticed Mother was wearing not one but two men's diamond pinky rings. She had had them reset for the fingers on her right hand. I never found out who had given them to her.

During Mother's visit with her sister Margie and brother-in-law Harry in Palm Springs, California, they were at the dinner table when two masked robbers entered the house. At gun point, the elders were told to lie down on the floor. Indignant, Mother yelled back that her younger sister was too old to lie on the floor, so the robbers allowed the three to stay seated. The robbers took Mother's jewelry, including the two diamond rings. Mother flew home the next day, still in shock. Sally insisted Mother's fear of being shot disoriented Mother for weeks.

After Mother died, Chris found a large collection of Mother's costume jewelry. We gave the necklaces to Mother's care center aides as mementoes for taking care of her. I did find some pieces of real jewelry we had never seen her wear: a soft pink jade necklace, a seed-pearl bracelet, and a diamond and sapphire watch. My biggest surprise was finding a pair of costume earrings I had given her for Christmas when I was six. I remember choosing them, with Daddy's help, at Reading's Heather Shop, her favorite up-scale store owned by her dear friend Rosie.

• A "REAL" MYTH •

The family's most thrilling myth-story described Mother capturing a German spy. The story began when she returned home from a trip to Germany with Daddy in 1938, a year after I was born. They were close to Punches Run, but it was late. They decided to eat dinner and spend one more night at an inn in Kutztown. No one seemed worried about the threat Germany posed, particularly in the years since Hitler began his move toward Nazi dictatorship. But Germany was already planning to send U-boats to prowl our East coast. Years later, I wrote this semi-fictional vignette based on the family's telling and retelling of the story.

Tripping Over a Spy

She crossed her right leg over her left with a swish of silk, seamed stockings, lifting her dress over her thighs to accommodate the relaxed pose, knowing her legs and ankles would show to their advantage. She cocked her head and asked for a light, placing her cigarette holder in her mouth, leaning forward just enough so he could smell her perfumed hair. He obliged and lit her Pall Mall. She inhaled deeply and blew smoke to the left. Thanking him with a smile, she watched his reaction. Satisfied, she stood up and walked over to the bartender who was mixing drinks. She knew the strange man's eyes were on her, watching the curves of her body through the movement of her dress, enjoying the softness of her back revealed through the filmy layers of chiffon.

She beckoned to the bartender and put her mouth close to his ear. After giving her order, she turned and faced the man who was sitting in the lounge chair while she put her elbows on the bar. Again, her faint smile. Then she sauntered back and returned to the chair opposite him.

The drinks appeared on a small tray. She took the nearest one, clicked glasses with the man, and drank deeply. Hers had bubbles drifting to the top of a champagne flute while his wide glass contained deep caramel-colored Scotch on the rocks with a twist.

Intrigued by his accent, she described her recent trip to Germany from which she was just returning. She guessed right. He loved the huge stone cathedrals and beautiful gardens she'd visited. He, too, loved the cuckoo-clock characters of one church in Berleburg, Westphalia. They shared laughter at the absurdity of the two stiff, wooden figures, a woman and man, who popped out of the clock's tall tower, extending greetings with their outstretched arms, their hands holding beer steins. Another set of drinks came. They polished off their first drinks, placed the empty glasses on the tray, and took new ones.

In a low voice, she spoke of her visits to a few major cities, then recounted going out to the country to see pine forests known for their straight rows of conifers. She said her property in Pennsylvania replicated these pine forests. She exuberantly praised the Germans for having forestry technology from which she benefitted. She spoke of seeing farmers in the countryside, marching in small groups in the woods. On their shoulders they carried shovels, picks, and rakes as if they were guns. She murmured something about preparing for war. He nodded knowingly. Another round of drinks.

She took her time, asking a few simple questions, leaning toward him, showing her interest in him, his family, and his line of work. He began to speak freely, the caramel liquid drowning his inhibitions. This American Marlene Deitrich — so interested in Germany, so beautiful, intelligent, alluring, and elusive. He could not resist her as he planned ways to seduce her, get her drunk enough so they might sleep together.

Despite his attempt to hide his drunkenness, his words slurred; unaware of what he said, he mumbled, smiling through half-opened eyes. Another round of drinks.

He felt good, even happy. He barely noticed the bartender helping him to his feet and guiding him to his room. Hazily, he saw her standing at his bedroom door, thinking she would soon disrobe him and herself. He smiled and closed his eyes.

A few hours later, three FBI agents entered his room. She stood in the shadows of the door, not visible to him, making the identification. He was taken away in the dead of night, still drunk, only to learn later his spying career had come to an abrupt end.

Tired, my Mother slipped into my Father's bed for a few hours of sleep before they set off for home the next day.

PART SIX

Director

Spiderweb window

CHAPTER SIXTEEN
Washington Years

• MOVING ON •

Given Mother's devotion to her work, Daddy's need to escape his business failure, and Kit Brown's willingness to offer him consolation, Daddy went to Reno for a quickie divorce in 1952, returning home to marry "Black Widow" Kit. Mother was 50 years old.

When Mother and Daddy were hashing out their divorce settlement, he balked at continuing to pay for private school and college. Extolling the advantages of staying nearby, Daddy asked if I would be willing to finish at a Reading public high school and then matriculate to a small local college. When I mentioned Daddy's supplication to Mother, she would not hear of it. Daddy agreed to pay. Mother and I assumed Kit had tried to cut Daddy's expenses, so that she'd have more money for herself.

The animosity between the two women poisoned the fabric of our family. After Daddy divorced her, Mother never remarried, perhaps because she felt her father and Daddy had both betrayed her. Her heart had no room for trust or forgiveness. At the same time, she grieved the loss of the two most important men in her life. In order to protect herself, she fiercely exhibited her independence, even though she believed an unmarried woman held no status. Such were the conflicts and contradictions she lived with.

• NEW HOMES •

After the divorce, Mother, Chris, and I had to leave Punches Run.

Kit did not want anyone associated with Mother visiting or staying at "The Place." Daddy quietly complied. Kit invited Daddy's four older children to Punches Run, but never Mother's three children. Mother insisted that we call Daddy once or twice a year to arrange to see him, but he made no effort to stay connected. Hurt and sad, we plunged into a life without him.

Mother discovered a house that reminded us of Punches Run — not a castle but a home surrounded by woods. Sally had moved to a job in California, and although Chris and I were home only for school vacations, we loved the house and hoped she'd buy it to soften the harsh move. But Mother needed to save money, so she bought a rather ugly place in a suburb of Reading until she could plan where to go next.

During our last year in Reading, a kind, gentle man — clearly smitten by Mother — often came for dinner, but Mother apparently wasn't ready for any relationship, a pattern she repeated for years to come. He eventually married someone else, but he and Mother remained friends.

Because Daddy's settlement was not enough to support the three of us, Mother had to find a job. Given her aviation connections in Washington, she began interviewing and following leads. In 1953, at the age of 51, she secured an important and demanding job. At first, she rented an apartment in Georgetown and commuted from Reading when we were home during the summer. As the job took hold, and she knew she was going to work in Washington permanently, she bought a house in Georgetown where the three of us lived until Chris and I left to get married. Mother lived there until she retired in her early 70s. For 40 years, she remained in the metropolitan Washington area.

• PREPARING FOR WWIII •

Various newspapers offered details about Frannie's new responsibilities, capturing stories about the last half of her life. She had found the perfect job as director of general aviation, leading a division of the Defense Air Transportation Administration (DATA) of the U.S. Department of Commerce. Responsible for planning the mobilization of commercial and private planes in case of a national emergency (a euphemism for "war"), she counted on these planes to reinforce and support military war efforts. Overall, she was responsible for the Civil Air Reserve Fleet and the National Emergency Airlift Plan.

One tattered newspaper clipping, with no date and no source, begins with a headline in bold caps: OVER ENTIRE U.S. WOMAN HEADS AIR MOBILIZATION. It reads,

> Hers is a Herculean job of planning for the mobilization of civil aviation — air carriers, corporative aircraft, and light planes — for defense. Since taking the job, Mrs. Nolde has directed the organization of these branches of DATA: The Civil Reserve Air Flight — made up of commercial airships. The War Air Service Pattern — commercial transports. And the National Emergency Defense Air Lift — civilian planes.
>
> Mrs. Nolde said, "All of this has been going on very quietly, but I think it would be reassuring to Americans to know that the work is being done. ... The bottleneck, of course, is manpower," said Mrs. Nolde. "We have just completed a survey which showed the number of people we would need in skilled categories to keep planes flying in an emergency. This deficit is about 23,000 persons. We haven't found a solution for this problem yet, but we are working with leaders of the reserve program to see if we could have some reservists assigned to us if war should break out."

Given the need for "persons" to fly, Frannie clearly had women in mind. Under the headline, "Adept Aviatrix Appointed as Consultant to DATA." *The Evening Star* in D.C. reported,

> Mrs. Nolde was both surprised and elated to be selected for the job. "I think it's a recognition of women in aviation," she happily commented in an interview. "In fact, I think this may be taken as an indication that the Eisenhower policy of putting qualified women in responsible positions is being followed by the Department of Commerce."
>
> Her chief assignment will be to work out plans for an adequate manpower reserve to assure successful operation of the Civil Reserve Air Fleet. Mrs. Nolde has high praise for the spirit of cooperation between the military, civilian, and government officials as they work on this mammoth joint operation.
>
> One of the biggest parts of the job confronting her will be to further develop DATA's plan for mobilization of 1,800 corporation-owned aircraft in time of attack. These planes will fly nurses, doctors, supplies, blankets and other first aid equipment in event of disaster. There are 1,200 individually owned light aircraft which will be drafted into service. Mrs. Nolde's other duties will include directing mobilization in the fields of manpower, training, noncarrier aviation, overhauling and maintenance and replacement parts.

As in many newspaper articles, *The Evening Star* focused on her christening her plane *Reposa*: "Laughingly she remarked, 'You really need it, especially after bringing up seven children as I've done.'"

The Washington Post, in July of 1953, began with the headlines: "Takes Appointment in Stride. NEW DESK JOB FAILS TO CLIP HER WINGS." The article reviewed her aviation career, saying she had 4,500 flying hours in the "wide blue yonder."

The paper continues, "She is used to doing a variety of jobs ably and simultaneously." In describing her commute from Reading to Washington and back, she speaks of debarking from her plane and having to go to her desk job by taxi, calling the car ride "... the only dangerous part of the trip."

"This petite, blue-eyed blonde says, 'The days of flying helmets and goggles for pilots is long since past. I always fly my plane, except on Civil Air Patrol missions, in something like this.' This, on the day in question, being a natural shantung suit, white straw hat, tan and white high-heeled shoes."

Then, the reporter emphasized in boldface:

> **One of the things she finds most challenging about her latest job is the chance it will give her to develop plans for training women in various aspects of aviation. She hopes to launch a junior college and university air program for women.**
>
> In the field of communications — radio and control tower maintenance, and airport management — the frontiers are expanding continually for women, she says. The Air Force trains women for those jobs and others they can do in civil aviation, among them aerial photography and meteorology. Frances Nolde recommends business and engineering training as musts for college girls seriously interested in aviation as a career. Gradually, masculine prejudice against women flyers and as airport operations personnel is breaking down, she finds, although the U.S. Air Force, unlike that of several European nations, will not permit women to fly its planes. Despite the excellent record of women ferry pilots during World War II, the "women are so fragile" myth still lives on Capitol Hill.

Representing the strength of women in aviation, Frannie attended Ninety-Nines meetings regularly and helped aero clubs get started. She was vice-president of the National Aeronautic Association and a delegate several times to the *Federation Aeronautique Internationale* (FAI). She traveled to the Hague, Madrid, and Turkey to represent America at FAI meetings. She enjoyed traveling abroad.

In 1954, a *Richmond Times Dispatch* headline reveals, "Woman Aviator Visits Richmond; Has Ambition to Fly Jet Planes." It goes on to say, "Mrs. Nolde started flying to keep ahead of the children, and now is nursing an ambition to try out jets." I remember her telling me of her hope, but the demands of her job made it impossible.

When she moved to D.C., she placed *Reposa VII* with an aviation service in Maryland, and eventually sold a half share to someone who would keep the plane in the air and help with maintenance fees. When Frannie finally sold her share in *Reposa VII*, she stoically admitted she would never again enjoy the thrill of flying.

CHAPTER SEVENTEEN

Private Life

• FRIENDSHIPS •

Frannie made long-standing friendships in Washington and had many male admirers who came to her Georgetown house for cocktails before going home to their families. She engaged her friends with her public persona, not revealing her more critical nature that family members had come to know.

She kept close ties with many female pilots of her era, particularly Blanche Noyes, Jean Howard, Betty Warnock, Mrs. Abbot Johnson, and Vi Delp, Frannie's co-pilot in her second Powder Puff Derby.

Throughout her life, Mother kept a trove of letters from friends and relatives. When she was 60, a favorite friend wrote, "Hi-ho, Loveliness." Then he asked about Sally: "What does she look like at this point? Naturally she should be beautiful…."

The same year, another friend's letter says: "Connie fell in love with you, your gracious manner, your vibrancy, your smart way of dressing and your lovely looks. I'll never know how you do it — working at high pitch every minute and never losing one ounce of glamour. Whenever I see you I get inspired…."

Dressed in her best, and beautifully coifed, she was in her element when posing for pictures with Pat Nixon, Nancy Reagan, Hubert Humphrey, and other important dignitaries.

Mother was courted by a handful of beaux and, no doubt, received proposals. When I was in college, she said a man had carried her

Dressed for socializing with her aviator friend Blanch Noyes (left)

to her boudoir, and she had rebuffed him. Did she really want me to know about her personal life or make me her confidant? Her blunt revelation turned me away.

She remained well-coifed, beautifully dressed, elegant, and energetic. I remember her arriving in a gentleman's open convertible at my college for a rare visit. I could hear her hearty and melodious laughter well before she reached my dorm. She had enchanted this wealthy fellow, who, she told me, held no status and was too crude for her taste, not of the right upbringing. This man didn't hang around for long; she dropped him.

• HER "GROUPIE" •

After leaving Punches Run for Georgetown, Mother developed another interest, most likely at the suggestion of Daly King, a psychologist and mystery writer whom she visited often in Bermuda. In the '30s and '40s, Daly participated in a New York Harlem group that studied two mystics: Gurdjieff, an esoteric Greek-Armenian spiritual teacher, and Ouspensky, a Russian philosopher/writer and Gurdjieff follower.

On a weekly basis, she joined her discussion "groupie" and began studying Gurdjieff and Ouspensky. Gurdjieff believed education and conditioning make most of us spend our lives as unconscious automatons. Ouspensky wrote esoteric pieces about Gurdjieff's teachings, particularly *In Search of the Miraculous* and *The Fourth Way,* which Mother summed up as, "When we die, we go to the other side of the moon." Did she believe our spirits go to the dark side of the moon, where they hang out, waiting to learn about the next step? She evidently wanted to believe she would live on in some form.

During my senior year at college, when my a cappella singing group was performing at Carnegie Hall, Mother invited my fiancé and me to attend a program of Dervish dances performed by Sufis. The dancers presented feats of incredible physical endurance that demanded extraordinary concentration, such as whirling hundreds of times non-stop, like ballet dancers twirling around and around on just one foot. Mother never explained why she wanted us to have this experience beyond "Come and see," but I imagine she saw a form of ultimate control and spiritual transcendence in the trance-like dancing.

Her intellect was keen enough for the search, but she ended up judging the people studying alongside her, rather than probing the meaning of the material. Daly King wrote her long, single-spaced typed letters outlining the conflicts and schisms among the many people and groups around the world, mirroring the final break between Ouspensky and Gurdjieff themselves. Daly told her to stay with the group if she was getting enough out of it. When she stopped attending her "groupie," she simply said the people were all very "queer and peculiar." There was more to it than that. She had lost the tolerance of others she had when I was a child.

CHAPTER EIGHTEEN
Breaking Away

As I grew older, a feeling of distrust kept me at a distance from Mother. She could use sweet talk and perform a kind act, and then belittle the person with criticism behind their back. That behavior made me wary of her doing the same to me. It did happen. Shortly after I was accepted into college, I overhead her speaking to a friend on the phone. She said she wished I had selected Vassar. Although it was a college I had never considered, I understood she liked the status symbol of Vassar.

In following mother's social values, I lost touch with my intuition and inner voice. From the ages of 13 to 28, I did all the "right" things. I attended a "good" girls' boarding school, a "good" all-women's college; I followed all the "good" social requirements, joined the "good" Boston clubs, and I entered a "good" marriage. Later, I asked myself, "Is this it? Is this all there is?" At first, I didn't realize I had been trying to be someone I wasn't. I had told myself I was trying out different hats to learn which one fit. None of them fit because they belonged to someone else, not me. It took a jolt to recalibrate myself.

The jolt was my divorce. I re-examined my childhood experience of walking in the Pennsylvania woods and communing with Nature. I knew I had to return to the girl who had remained inside me, allowing her to gradually express herself and grow up alongside the 28-year-old. I felt ecstatic and deliriously happy to reconnect with what I knew to be true. It didn't take long to weave the threads and heal the disparate parts of myself into one whole self.

Finally, I could raise my children with an open, loving heart that would benefit the three of us. Finally, I could look at the nighttime sky, marvel at the mystery, and know life was as it should be, mistakes and all. My daughters Laurel and Lexi are now passing these values and principles on to their own children. Laurel is a seeker on a spiritual path; Lexi is an advocate for equity and justice.

My second marriage later in life reflects the qualities I yearned for. Our covenant says: *We commit to leading balanced lives with a vital appreciation of the flavor and wonder of our differences. Each day we will strive to see one another freshly, as if for the first time. With patience and kindness, we will make time to speak openly and honestly, to listen to each other with a desire to understand. With open hearts and minds, we accept one another unconditionally.*

PART SEVEN

Enigma

CHAPTER NINETEEN
Dramatic Shifts

• SEPARATION •

Over time, Frannie changed. Once kind, generous, and magnanimous, she gradually became an ultra-conservative: an argumentative Republican, John Bircher, and supporter of Barry Goldwater. Why did Mother turn against her better nature as she aged? Most likely the answer lies in Daddy's divorcing her at a point in her life when she was flourishing. Despite their clashes, it was not a mutual decision.

The impact of being thrown out of Punches Run affected her deeply. She lost social status, disposable income for her expensive taste in clothes and belongings, and a way of life that included large cocktail parties, private planes, and taking "junkets" whenever and wherever she wanted, flying at will. So, she had to go to work, a daunting reality as she took on huge responsibilities in preparing private aviation for a possible third world war.

During this time, most of our conversations led her to harsh judgments. As she hardened, she didn't grasp the insidiousness of her inflexibility. To me, she became a different person and a very different mother.

After my first husband and I had lived and worked in West Africa for three years, I returned home alone to have my first child. While I was living with Mother, she told me she had recently read a book that proved Black people had smaller, inferior brains. She then announced that all Nigerians should be put on a boat, sent out to sea, and blown up because they were worthless and used resources that could be put to better use.

Shocked and dumbfounded, I walked out of the room. I didn't try to argue; I knew I would not make headway. I couldn't even find the appropriate words to condemn racism and bigotry. Having enjoyed the company of many Nigerians and Cameroonians while I lived in their countries, and having received respect and affection for being an American, I didn't know where to start. I was then a woman of 25, still finding my way in the world. Today, I would approach her racism differently. Mother's disrespect and lack of interest in the relationships I had developed in West Africa hurt me. Not only was her flat-out racism loud and clear, so was her inability to hear her own words.

After that incident, I realized I had to protect myself. The slights and hurts were mounting, and I knew I must limit my interactions with Mother. When I was with her, I focused on the basics of life, revealing nothing, not exposing myself emotionally or allowing her to hurt me. Ironically, following the pattern she began, I started the process of disconnecting, creating a self-imposed, protective wall.

• DECLINE •

After she retired from the Department of Commerce in her early 70s, Mother successfully trained as a real estate agent and began work of a different kind. Her new career ended when she had a stroke during the removal of a tumor on the outside of her lung, a tumor she denied existed.

The stroke affected her left side and impaired her speech. For almost two weeks, the surgeon ignored her odd post-op behavior, even though Sally and Chris spoke with him about it. She appeared as if she were still sedated. For reasons we still don't understand, the surgeon squandered precious time by ignoring the mysterious symptoms.

Unbeknownst to us, Mother had sneaked a flask into her hospital room and drank Scotch the night before the operation. When given anesthesia, she suffered a stroke. Her nurse said Mother's room had a strong smell of alcohol and asked us point blank: "Is your mother an alcoholic?" When I asked Mother why the room smelled of alcohol, she replied she must have spilled her flask.

No doubt, Mother was an alcoholic. Over the years, she would periodically "go on the wagon," and all too often say, "I've fallen off the wagon." As a teenager, I had become used to her needing more than one Scotch before dinner. Years later, after cocktails with friends, she drove my daughters and me home on the wrong side of the road. I had to scream to get her to avoid oncoming cars.

After her stroke, however, she barely engaged in social conversations. She lost interest in the fiery exchanges she had always enjoyed. Occasionally her anger and frustration at being incapacitated spewed out, and she'd have a minor tantrum. That would pass, and she'd return to her immobilized self. Her declining years seemed mired in hidden torment.

She declined to come to the Boston area, where I had offered to look after her. She was not interested because she knew no one, and it was not a "cosmopolitan" enough setting. Eventually, Mother lived in several life-care centers in the D.C. area. When she turned 90, she returned to Reading to live in a care center with old-time friends. But she didn't like it and returned to a facility in Bethesda, Maryland, where she died at the age of 93.

CHAPTER TWENTY

Reflections

As I look back, I remember just one adult conversation with Mother. Before her stroke, with no one else around at her breakfast table, she began to talk about herself. I think she wanted to express her regrets and mistakes in dealing with Daddy and not being able to save her marriage. She wished she and I could have maintained the sweet relationship we had had when I was a little girl. She realized that she drove some of her stepchildren away. And she wished she could undo any harm she had caused. Whatever she said and however she said it, I sensed her humanity, her struggles, her attempts to be a kind person, and her awareness of her failures, all bound up in a surprising talk. Although this one conversation could not heal all hurts, I felt we could engage more peacefully.

Much later, after she had been hospitalized for congestive heart failure, I left work for a week to care for her in Washington. Early one morning, when getting ready to leave, I stood by her bedside to say goodbye. She asked me point blank if I thought she were dying.

From my hospice training and work, I knew I should deflect the question and turn it back to her. Instead, I answered truthfully. "No, Mother, I don't think you are dying. Do you?"

She shook her head: No. Then, she turned to me and said, "I haven't been very nice, have I?"

I replied, "No, you haven't." I took her hand and squeezed it, thinking of how she had barked at me, complained incessantly about her illness as if it were my fault, demanded I react faster, and criticized me for not doing enough. My eyes welled up. I heard and accepted her apology.

A taxi waited outside, an echo of her leaving my fifth-grade play. I regret I didn't engage her further with, "Tell me what you think happens after you die?" I never asked and never learned her answer. Still the dark side of the moon?

• ROLE MODELS •

Frannie was a complex woman. I wonder if the combination of her beauty and intelligence led to a kind of egocentricity that prevented her from finding personal happiness. Perhaps she gave in to the need to be loved and adored by others rather than to take care of her inner self, her deep soul. I don't know how she felt about these matters at the end of her life. By that time, she had lost her great strength to engage in life.

Nevertheless, she had made her mark. Ahead of her time — along with a small number of women pilots in the '40s and early '50s — she devoted her life to aviation. And in the following decades, she served the nation as a strategic leader. Believing women were smart and able to achieve great things, she wanted them to play a key role in aviation. Her effort to propel young women into aviation inspired women pilots to succeed.

She modeled for all women that they could reach whatever they set out to accomplish. She presented a positive view of herself: confidence, the ability to get things done, and the will to complete difficult tasks. Moreover, she had a sense of humor; she didn't take herself too seriously. Whenever she told us something corny, she would hold up her right arm and then pretend to bite along it, as if it were an ear of corn. We'd all laugh at the family joke.

Because of her, I have never questioned my ability to meet a new challenge. Because of her, I know women are powerful and smart, strong-minded and capable, gracious and caring, gorgeous in their own way, and generous. She showed me that women can be leaders who demonstrate courage, independence, resourcefulness, agility, and dedication to their goals and dreams.

Because of Mother, I have believed I could do anything important and worth the effort. Never did I deal with low self-esteem or fear I didn't have the necessary "credentials." Like Mother, I entered territories usually dominated by men. In those roles, I never doubted my ability and good will to make life a little bit better or easier for others, especially women.

For a long while, I had forgotten a second role model I had known as a child. As I began studying to become a psychotherapist, I remembered that when I was a young girl, Daddy spoiled me with surprises, gifts he brought home every time he traveled for business to San Francisco, New York City, New Orleans, Chicago, or Boston. Sometimes it would be pralines from New Orleans (my favorite), trinkets from different places, or books.

One treasured book, *Jane Addams, Little Lame Girl,* tells a true story about a sickly girl who couldn't join others in school or at play. When she grew up, however, she founded Hull House, a settlement home in Chicago for poor, immigrant women, helping them join American culture, learn English, and find jobs. She became the first female president of the National Conference of Social Work. She was a suffragette, a co-founder of the ACLU, and the second woman to receive the Nobel Peace Prize. She taught me to open my heart to serving others.

When my thoughts turn to Mother, I accept the major differences between us. Still, from my early days growing up at Punches Run, from the constant love from her and Daddy, and from early morning walks in the woods, I learned to have reverence for Nature and its life-sustaining gifts. I learned that life is a mystery with no answers, and we are protected by love, the most sustaining quality in life.

• SHE LOOKED TO THE SKY •

A few days after Mother died, Chris wrote a tribute to her, and Chris' wife Sylvia, who worked for Pennsylvania Senator Arlan Specter, gave it to the Senator to read on the floor of Congress. The piece is printed in the Congressional Record of October 26, 1995 and appears in the Appendix.

I began to go through the few boxes of things she had saved. Each time she had moved, Sally had helped Mother decide what to keep and what to jettison. The boxes held many letters from old friends, some from the early '20s, some written by Daddy to his older children in the '30s and '40s, some from Jeanne, and some from me. She kept photographs, both old and new, plus news about family members' accomplishments, particularly those of Chris. And she kept her awards, citations, and a pile of newspaper clippings. I discovered the photos of her growing up in Deposit, New York, when cars were just being manufactured and family members spent time with one another. I saw Mother's face, soft and happy.

When I turned 50, and she was 85, I wrote her a letter of appreciation which I found she had kept. I wanted her to know that the love she gave me as a child had stood up well in my life, that her leadership roles led me to my own, and that her dedication to education paid it forward. I mentioned loving her laughter and jokes.

Because she never acknowledged the letter, I was astounded to find she also had kept a copy of a poem I had written for her 90th birthday:

A Woman Ahead of Her Time

You were a woman ahead of your time.
With your well-heeled pumps on the wing of your plane,
Your silk scarves and well-fitted hats flying in the winds
Of powdery puffs, or perhaps
Caught in the side-car as you scooted back to Punches-on-the-Run,
You were a woman ahead of your time.

An actress ahead of your time.
Your English accent confounding all who heard,
You caught a German spy with your wily wiles,
Your role of multifaceted, many-sided star.
You championed the less fortunate and gave to those in need.
And ran a complex household while Deposit honored your flying career with an airport by name.

You were a woman ahead of your time.
You could have been President of the United States.
You could have run your own business.
You could have been most anything.
You simply chose to be
A woman ahead of her time.

REPOSA VI
Ryan Navion SUPER 260

Acknowledgments

The writing of this book started in a roundabout way. An acquaintance, Kay Robert, sent mutual friends an amusing book about Pancho Barnes, a female, barnstorming pilot from the '20s and '30s; our friends shared the book with me. I mentioned to Kay that my mother had been a pilot, too. She Googled my mother's name and wrote me, "Someone ought to write a book about your mother." That did it!

From the start, family members — both immediate and extended — encouraged me and showed their interest. Some read an early version, telling me how the story moved and instructed them. Their comments kept me going. When I gave updates, they listened and responded with questions, giving me a boost. I knew I could count on them for thoughtful responses. I remain grateful for their support.

My brother Chris expressed his gratitude for my effort to share our mother's story. We have a mutual understanding of the beauty, complexity, dynamic, pain, and patterns of our family history. Chris showed me his love through his kindness and generosity during the writing process.

For safekeeping, I had already sent some family documents to Berks County Historical Society and the archivist at the Nolde Forest Environmental Education Center. When I began writing in earnest, I relied on both institutions to help me understand how local history influenced my family and my mother.

When I went through my box of Mother's newspaper stories, I found she had clipped off dates and newspaper names, and her collection of photos seldom identified the names of people. The newspapers were mostly accurate but frequently failed to identify their sources. Thus, I apologize and take responsibility for any mistakes. Any blame for factual errors, omissions, or failures in emphasis belong to me.

ACKNOWLEDGMENTS

I have many people to thank and am endlessly grateful to them.

Hugh Fortmiller, writer/editor and magnanimous master English teacher, turned my poorly worded effort into a piece worth reading. This is as much his book as it is mine. As my husband and friend, he helped me feel I was accomplishing my goal of portraying Mother as a complicated, determined woman who wanted to make a difference in the world of aviation.

Jeanne Abboud, our wise, creative book designer, graced our lives by presenting the varied material elegantly. Without pressure, she joyfully encouraged us to make sure the book said all we felt it should say.

David Livesey, a printing master and friend, knew better than anyone how to bring Jeanne's design to life. I am grateful for their partnership.

Maria Lindberg, copy editor, to whom I'm endlessly grateful for picking up the many overlooked inconsistencies and for making many suggestions that improved the flow and clarity of the book.

Barbie Wolfenden, a friend, writer, and teacher of memoirs, encouraged me and lent me a handful of editing and publishing books. She gave my manuscript a thorough reading and offered many suggestions.

Kathleen Lang, a New England friend who I discovered had grown up in Reading, PA, sent me enlightening articles from the Historical Review of Berks County, particularly "Hans Nolde: The First Berks Countian to Cross the Atlantic by Air."

Dick Ferarro, a friend and retired American Airlines pilot, described how a pilot of a small plane would land at a local, municipal airport, giving authenticity to the story "Broken Wing."

Lisa Adams, archival assistant at Berks History Center, spent hours on my behalf searching for papers and articles about Mother's life during the 1940s and early '50s.

Nolde Forest Environmental Education Center: Director **Brent M. Erb** welcomed and encouraged my use of the Center for information and photographs; many beautiful photographs are his. I have high regard for staff members **Sarah Presogna** and **Ashalisett Carabello** who cheerfully responded to my many requests.

Hallie Vaughan, a women's history enthusiast, instructor, reenactor, and longtime volunteer at the Berks History Center, portrayed the life of Frannie at a "Famous Ladies" Tea at the Nolde Mansion. During National Women's History Month, she created a blog about Frannie, "The Woman with Wings." She shared her research and the photos of her portrayal of Frannie as a CAP Captain.

Sime B. Bertolet sent me information about how his dad Sime, Frannie's close friend, had started Reading Aviation Service. I babysat for young Sime when he was an infant.

George Brizek, a member of the Pennsylvania branch of the Civil Air Patrol, made sure my brother and I were present when the CAP received the Congressional Medal of Honor. He also shared information about Mother that he discovered when preparing for the event in Washington.

Col. Frank Blazich, Jr., Civil Air Patrol National Historian, was helpful in identifying my mother's roles with the CAP and providing a significant CAP illustration.

Jan Mapes, a distant cousin through the Dean-Wilcox lineage, and a volunteer for the Deposit, New York, Historical Society, shared information about the town and family history. To discover we are related is a pure delight.

Heather Allison Waters and **Ronald L. Theile,** deans of advancement, and **Nicole Westerdahl,** librarian, at Syracuse University, searched early 1900s records for information on Mother's university career. They responded with genuine interest.

Emily. S. Cole, as director of alumni engagement, Oberlin Alumni Association, gave me Mother's attendance dates and offered assistance.

Larry Groebe, founder of the Generic Radio Workshop in Dallas, Texas, encouraged me to print as "fair use" the excerpt from "Gloria Gay's Affairs."

Appendix

AWARDS AND APPOINTMENTS:

1. 1942: Appointed Commander of Pennsylvania wing of the Civil Air Patrol.

2. 1948: Winner of the Powder Puff Derby, the Jacqueline Cochran Intercontinental All-Women's Race, Palm Springs, California to Miami, Florida.

3. 1949: Placed third, Powder Puff Derby, Montreal to Miami.

4. 1949: Named a commissioner of the Reading Airport, Reading, PA, where she was responsible for the airport operation and maintenance. This position helped her change the name to the *General Karl A. Spaatz Airfield* in 1951.

5. 1950: Honored by the Deposit, New York Air Show dedication to Frances Dean Wilcox Nolde.

6. 1951: Became a full colonel in the Civil Air Patrol as the first national director of the CAP's women's program. This job called for developing and expanding the program, with special emphasis on girl cadet activities.

7. 1951: Received the honor of having the Deposit, New York, airport named *The Frances Wilcox Nolde Airport.*

8. 1952: Became Delegate to the *Federation Aeronautique Internationale (FAI)* in Madrid, again in 1953 at the Hague, and later in Turkey.

9. 1953: Became Director of General Aviation, leading a division of the Defense Air Transportation Administration of the U.S. Department of Commerce, responsible for the Civil Air Reserve Fleet and National Emergency Airlift Plan.

10. Board member of:

- Reading, PA, Junior League
- Governors and Membership Chairman of National Aviation Club

11. Accomplishments as an aviator:

- Honorary member of Reading Aero Club (1949)
- Distinguished Citizen's Award for Leadership in the Advancement of Aviation, 1950, Altrusa International Organization
- Vice president, National Aeronautic Association
- Delegate to *Federation Aeronautique Internationale* (FAI)
- Vice president, FAI Economic Technical Commission
- Commissioner of Reading, PA, Airport
- Governor, Ninety-Nines (99s, an international organization of women pilots) and Vice President of its Contest Division
- Vice President and Treasurer, Aero Club of Washington, D.C.
- Member, President's Women's Advisory Committee on Aviation
- Member, American Newspaper Women's Clubs

To find more biographical information, go to *Who's Who in American Aviation* and *Who's Who of American Women.*

THE DERBY

The Powder Puff Derby was frequently mentioned in the television series *The Astronaut Wives Club (2015).*

THREE-YEAR RECORD: POWDER PUFF DERBY

The Powder Puff Derby results were broadcast in a variety of ways: statistics, photographs of contestants, and summaries. The last three years of the 1940s included Frannie's 1948 victory.

Year	**From/To**	**Miles**	**Aircraft**	**Pilot/Co-Pilot Winner**
1947	Palm Springs/Tampa	2242	Ercoupe	Carolyn West/ Beatrice Medes
1948	Palm Springs/Miami	2540	Navion	Frances Nolde
1949	San Diego/Miami	2544	Piper Clipper	Laurette Foy/ Sue Kindred

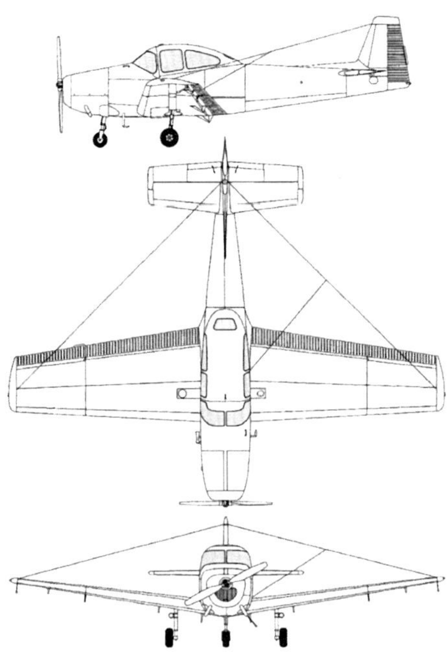

THE FOUNDING OF WHANDER FIELD, READING, PA

Whander field was developed as a true community project without any federal or state subsidy. It was quite modest by today's standards — a single, very short (about 1200 ft.) grass runway which was adequate for the flying machines of the day. A swath of land had simply been cleared of weeds and bushes to provide the strip. It wasn't even level, and it had a small knoll at about the three-quarter point that acted a bit like a launching ramp for takeoffs. The name of the field was formed from the first letter of the last name of each of the Chamber of Commerce Aviation Committee members who immodestly decided to immortalize themselves. Sharing the same last initial, Messrs. Wolfinger and Wilson evidently claimed the first letter.

- W – John P. Wolfinger, Sr. and Thomas A. Wilson
- H – Fred A. Howard
- A – Arthur Arrowsmith
- N – Hans W. Nolde
- D – Harry Davis
- E – Paul O. Edelman
- R – R. K. G. Rice

FRANNIE'S FATHER'S TOWN BUDGET

MAYOR'S REPORT

President Wilcox Submits Report as President of Village.

RECEIPTS AND EXPENDITURES

The Village Budget. Estimates and Expenses for the Ensuing Year. Sidewalk Laid.

Deposit, N. Y., Feb. 21st, 1910.

To the Trustees of the Village of Deposit.

Gentlemen:

I herewith submit the following report, as President of the Village of Deposit, for the year 1909:

Owing to the financial situation that has existed in this locality for the past year it was deemed necessary to make the village budget this year as small as possible and consequently only a small amount of work was done on the streets, except sidewalks, which were put in very good condition by filling up spaces between where walks were already laid and making the line continuous;, also by laying some other pieces of walk which were much needed. Altogether there were laid about 900 feet as follows: 750 feet of 5-foot walk, 150 feet of 4-foot walk, 140 feet of Belgian bridge cross walk, 25 feet of 4-foot stone crossing 10 inches thick at Laurel Bank cemetery; also 35 feet of 6-foot sluice, 40 feet of 2-foot sluice, 90 feet of 1-foot sluice.

Fenders to guard against teams running off highways were put up on Second street and river road, making these thoroughfares much safer than formerly, and adding greatly to the appearance of the streets. Also raised walk on academy corner, Center and Second streets, and raised crosswalk North end Second street. and crosswalk on Second street at Monument street.

I estimate the expenses for the ensuing year as follows:

Highways	$3,500
Water	800
Street lighting	1,575
Coal	300
Police	500
Board of Health	500
Vital statistics	100
Village hall bond and interest	1,070
Insurance	50
Fire department	200
Assessors	40
Village hall	250
Exemptions and sidewalk certificates	300
Miscellaneous	500
Total	$9,685

One new street lamp has been installed on High street, near the residence of Miss Emma Demander.

About $400 worth of nice stone suitable for crushing for use on the streets is on the ground of the village lot. This is paid for and can be used by the incoming board of 1910.

The following pieces of sidewalk have been laid for which certificates have been issued: Andrew Ryan, 58 feet of 5-inch 5-foot walk, A. E. Kingsbury 51 feet of 5-inch 5-foot walk. A new substantial culvert was constructed at corner of Dean and Second streets and the northerly end of Wheeler street was improved by being raised and drained.

F. D. Wilcox,
President.

FRANCES W. NOLDE, PIONEER AVIATRIX

Mr. SPECTER. Mr. President, I was recently advised of the passing of a distinguished American, Frances W. Nolde, of Reading, PA. In addition to an illustrious career as a pioneer in aviation and in the theater, she is the mother of a distinguished Washingtonian, H. Christopher Nolde, who is the husband of another distinguished Washingtonian, Mrs. Sylvia Nolde, who was my Executive Assistant for almost 14 years after serving in a similar capacity with Senator Jacob Javits.

Mr. President, I wish to acknowledge the life of Frances W. Nolde with a brief recitation of her career for the CONGRESSIONAL RECORD.

Frances W. Nolde was a woman ahead of her time, whose life spanned nearly the entire 20th century. She made unique contributions to the field of aviation as a pilot, World War II Civil Air Patrol leader, visionary, and achiever, all the while raising a family of seven children, founding and directing a country day school, and receiving acclaim as a civic leader in her home community. Musically talented, with a flair for the dramatic, Mrs. Nolde had a budding career on stage and in radio.

Born in Deposit, NY, in 1902, she attended Oberlin Conservatory of Music and graduated from Syracuse University with a BA and BS in Music. She married Carlton Brown, who later became an accomplished Hollywood screen writer. Their marriage ended in divorce.

Frances lived in the New York City area and played in a hit Broadway musical "Lady Be Good," starring Fred Astaire in the 1920s, and starred in one of the first radio soap operas, under her stage name Gloria Gay.

Upon marrying a successful businessman, Hans W. Nolde, Frances moved to Reading, PA, where she was one of the first to combine career and family and became well known for civic and philanthropic activities. She was a board member of the Junior League and founded and directed The New School, and country day school.

A pioneer in aviation, Frances Nolde was one of the early women pilots, beginning in 1940. During World War II she commanded a Civil Air Patrol [CAP] courier base, flying cargo and key personnel for the war industries. She held the rank of full colonel, the highest allowable to women at that time, and was the first National Director of Women in Aviation for the CAP.

In 1948 she won the inaugural All-Women's Transcontinental Air Race—Powder Puff Derby—from Los Angeles to Miami.

The Distinguished Citizen's Award for Leadership in the Advancement of Aviation was presented in 1950 to her by the Altrusa International Organization.

Mrs. Nolde served as an Airport Commissioner and arranged with General Carl A. Spaatz and the U.S. Air Force to rename the Reading municipal Airport as the General Carl A. Spaatz Field.

She later became associated with the Reading Aviation Service and was Public Relations Director of Aviation Consultants, Inc.

Upon her divorce from Hans, she moved to the Washington, D.C., area where she lived for more than 40 years. During that time she was employed by the U.S. Department of Commerce as the Director of General Aviation in the Defense Air Transportation Administration. She was responsible for the Civil Air Reserve Fleet and the National Emergency Airlift Plan. Mrs. Nolde was a member of the American Newspaper Women's Clubs, the Top Flight Club, and the Ambassador's Club.

Her accomplishments and contributions include: vice-president National Aeronautics Association; delegate to Federation Aeronautique Internationale [FAI]; vice-president, FAI Economic Technical Commission; Governor 99's (International Organization of Women Pilots) and Vice President of its Contest Division; Vice President and Treasurer of Aero Club of Washington, DC.; Board of Governors and membership Chairman of National Aviation Club; member President's "Women's Advisory Committee on Aviation."

Mrs. Nolde held a commercial pilots rating, and logged more than 10,000 hours flying time over her outstanding aviation career. A full biography can be found in Who's Who In The World Of Aviation and also in Who's Who of American Women.

A long time resident of Bethesda, MD, Mrs. Nolde was 93 when she passed away on October 22. She is survived by her son, H. Christopher Nolde, of Washington, D.C.; daughter Sally Lutyens of Manset, ME; daughter Frances D. Nolde of Maynard, MA; 9 grandchildren and 8 great-grandchildren.

SENATOR CHARLES GRASSLEY

Mr. PRESSLER. Mr. President, CHUCK GRASSLEY is a man I much admire. Someday when I am out of here teaching a college course, I plan to cite CHUCK as a model Senator. He is not aware that I am placing this into the CONGRESSIONAL RECORD, and I am sure that he would protest the cost. However, I believe it is well worth it because he is probably the hardest working, most decent Senator around here. I often say, "CHUCK GRASSLEY is a real U.S. Senator. He is the real McCoy." He keeps a low profile but gets a lot done around here that never is credited to him. He is the type of a U.S. Senator that I particularly like. While some are retiring from this body with much fanfare, and others are holding press conferences about their achievements, CHUCK GRASSLEY keeps quietly working away. In the end, he will go down as one of the great U.S. Senators.

Mr. President, I ask unanimous consent to have printed in the RECORD a recent article that appeared in The Hill on October 25, 1995.

There being no objection, the article was ordered to be printed in the RECORD, as follows:

[From The Hill, Oct. 25, 1995]

SEN. CHARLES GRASSLEY—IOWA REPUBLICAN STANDS OUT AS WORKHORSE AMONG SENATE SHOWHORSES

(By Albert Eisele)

You can't get much more grassroots than Sen. Charles Grassley (R-Iowa).

Early this month, the 62-year-old crusader against federal waste was at the wheel of an International Harvester 1450 tractor, hauling a load of soybeans to a grain elevator near his family farm in northeastern Iowa.

The only working farmer in the Senate, Grassley interrupted his farming chores to issue a press release informing his constituents he had regained his Agriculture Committee seat, which he was forced to give up in January when committee assignments were redistributed after Republicans took control of the Senate.

But last week, Grassley was back in the Senate, behind the closed doors of the Finance Committee helping Republicans work out disagreements over their controversial $245-billion tax cut package, and then defending that package from Democratic criticism in full committee.

"If you're concerned about balancing the budget, you'll be for this program," Grassley declared as he and his GOP colleagues sent their historic tax package to the Senate floor as part of the even more historic budget reconciliation bill.

Then, using a metaphor appropriate to his Iowa origins and his parochial view of his role in the Senate, once described by Congressional Quarterly as "pigs and pork," Grassley said, "The people of this country are tired of living high on the hog, and not worrying about our children or grandchildren paying for it."

For the man who is the philosophical heir of the late Rep. H. R. Gross (R), the quintessential penny-pinching legislator whom Grassley succeeded in the House in 1974, it was a characteristic moment.

Never hailed as an intellectual giant or an inspiring orator, the easy-going third-term senator has made his name, and compiled a truly imposing campaign record, by balancing the needs of Iowa farmers and small businesses with the national yearning for fiscal discipline in government.

Despite one of the lowest profiles in the Senate, Grassley has managed, by stint of sheer hard work, country-bred political smarts and a low-octane ego, to place himself in the middle of the Senate debate over the big ticket issues of tax cuts, budget balancing and welfare reform at the heart of the Republican revolution.

As a member of the Finance Committee, the number two Republican on the Budget Committee behind Chairman Pete Domenici (R-N.M.), and a member of the House-Senate conference committee on welfare reform which holds its first meeting today, Grassley is perfectly positioned to add to his already impressive electoral achievements in Iowa, where he has never lost a race.

Elected to the state legislature while studying for a doctorate at the University of Iowa—he left school after he was elected and never returned—Grassley took over his family farm after his father died in 1960.

By 1974, when he won a narrow victory over a Democratic opponent to replace the retiring Rep. Gross, Grassley has bought additional acreage—it's now just under 600 acres—and turned the farm over to his son Robin, who still farms it, with weekend help from his father in the fall and spring.

Congressional Record, October 26, 1995

PHOTOGRAPHS, NEWPAPER CLIPPINGS, AND IMAGES

Unless otherwise noted, sources are identified as follows:

[Fam] Nolde Family Collection
[Int] Internet, Internet stock
[NFC] Nolde Forest Environmental Education Center, permission courtesy of Brent M. Erb, Director

Cover, front and back: [Fam]
Back flap, *The Author* [Fam]
Endpapers: *U.S. Map* [Int]

Pages:

2. *Tower* [Int]
10. *Frances…* [Fam]
12. *Fountain* [NFC], photo by Christine Mitchell
14. *Mayor's Report* [Fam]
16. *With Catherine* [Fam]
17. (top) *Bow,* (bottom) *Catherine & Elizabeth* [Fam]
18. *With Grandpa* [Fam]
19. *College years* [Fam]
22. *Fred/pacer* [Fam]
24. *Fred Astaire* [Fam]
25. *Adele Astaire* [Fam]
27. *Mother & Sally* [Fam], photo by Bachrach
28. *Gloria Gay* [Fam]
29. *Script* [Fam]
30. *Modeling silk crepe* [Fam]
31. *Marlene Dietrich* [Int]
32. *Fountain tiles* [NFC], photo by Christine Mitchell
34. *Newlyweds* [Fam]
36. *Daddy/axe* [Fam]
37. *The Place* [Fam]
38. *Porch* [Fam]
39. *Door handles* [NFC], photos by Brent M. Erb
44. *Forest path* [NFC], photo by Brent M. Erb
46. *Christmas tree* [NFC]
49. *Bobby's wedding* [Fam]
51. *Petunia* [Fam]

52. *Hansel & Gretel* [Fam]
66. *Deposit home* [Fam]
67. (top) *Riding,* (bottom) *Car* [Fam]
68. *Fox stole* [Fam]
69. *Appearance* [Fam]
72. *Tile detail* [NFC], photo by Brent M.Erb
74. *Johnny's wedding* [Fam]
75. *Wedding party* [Fam]
76. *Hans* [Fam]
77. *Frannie* [Fam]
81. *Jacob Nolde* [Int]
82. *"Single White Pine"* [Fam]
87. *Army Navy E* [Fam]
88. *Nolde & Horst* [Fam]
92. *In uniform* [Fam]
94. Reading Times [Fam]
99. *Waiting* [Fam]
105. *CAP logo* [Int]
108. *Captain Nolde* [Fam]
111. (left) *Amelia Earhart,* (right) *99s logo* [Int]
113. *New plane* [Fam]
115. *Pilots prepare* [Int]
118. *Waco stopover* [Fam]
120. *Mother Earhart* {Fam]
121. *Champ Greets Champ* [Fam]
122. *Frannie thrilled* [Fam]
123. *With her trophy* [Fam]
124. *Daddy's window* [NFC], photo by Brent M. Erb
125. *Celebrating* [Fam]
128. *The colonel* [Fam]
131. *Frannie teaches* [Fam]
132. *Woman's voice* [Fam]
133. *Military leaders* [Fam]
134. *With Gen. Beau* [Fam]
135. *Congressional Medal* [Int]
136. *CAP aircraft.* From a 1985 lithograph of an original painting by Donald Collins titled *CAP Coastal Aircraft, 1942-1943.* Permission to include the image courtesy of the Civil Air Patrol National Headquarters, Maxwell Air Force Base, Alabama. Special thanks to Colonel Frank Blazich, Jr., CAP National Historian.

139. *Giving Flying a Boost* [Fam]
140. (top) *Corsair,* (bottom) *War planes* [Int]
141. (top) *Parachutes,* (bottom) *Formation* [Int]
142. *Bevo trick* [Int]
143. *Bevo & Piper Cub* [Fam]
146. *Airport dedication* [Fam]
148. *The circle* [NFC], photo by Brent M. Erb
149. *With Gen. Spaatz* [Fam]
150. *Spaatz portrait* [Fam]
152. *Cow jumps over the moon* [NFC], photo by Brent M. Erb
154. *Hat box* [Fam]
157. *Rose quartz lamp* [Fam]
158. Time *cover* [Int]
161. *German village* [NFC], photo by Brent M. Erb
164. *Spiderweb window* [NFC], photo by Brent M. Erb
172. *Socializing* [Fam]
176. *Ferns* [NFC], photo by Brent M. Erb
178. *Misty path* [NFC]
187. *On* Reposa VI [Fam]
191. *Brass handle* [NFC], photo by Brent M. Erb
194. *Navion drawing* [Int], Maps Air Museum
195. *Ryan Navion drawing* [Int]
196. *Mayor's Report* [Fam]
197. *Congressional Record* [Int]
200. *Duck/grapes* [NFC], photo by Brent M. Erb
202. *Nolde Forest map* [NFC]
203. *Single white pine window* [NFC], photo by Brent M. Erb
204. *Scribe window* [NFC], photo by Brent M. Erb

REFERENCES & WORKS CITED

Ayers, Billie Pitman and Dees, Beth, *Superwoman Jacqueline Cochran,* 1st Books Library, 2001.

Blazich, Frank A., Jr., *An Honorable Place in American Air Power, Civil Air Patrol Coastal Patrol Operations, 1942-1943,* Air University Press, Maxwell Air Force Base, AL, 2020.

Brick, Kay, *Powder Puff Derby: The Record 1947-1977,* AWTAR, Inc., Fallbrook, CA, 1985.

Brooks-Pazmany, Kathleen, *United States Women in Aviation 1919-1929,* Smithsonian Institution Press, Washington, DC, 1991.

Douglas, Deborah G., *United States Women in Aviation 1940-1985,* Smithsonian Institution Press, Washington, DC, 1991.

Goreadingberks.com, search "Reading Air Show" for "Reading Aviation Service."

Nolde, John Jacob, *A Single White Pine, The Story of the Nolde Forest,* Department of Environmental Resources, Harrisburg, PA, 1970.

Oakes, Claudia M., *United States Women in Aviation 1930-1939,* Smithsonian Institution Press, Washington, DC, 1991.

Vaughan, Hallie, *A Woman with Wings: Frances Dean Wilcox Nolde,* berkshistorymysteries.wordpress.com, 2018.

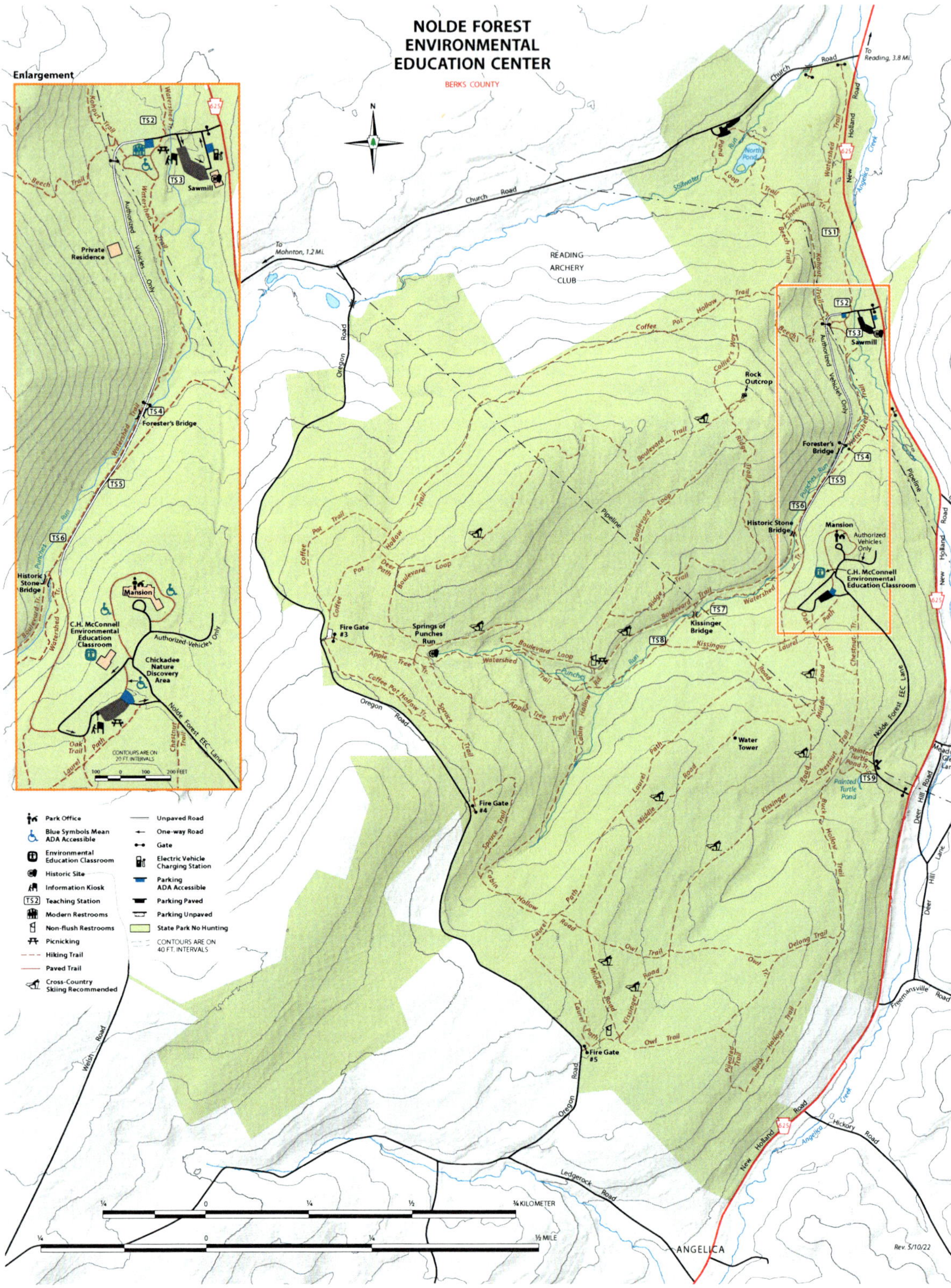
NOLDE FOREST
ENVIRONMENTAL
EDUCATION CENTER
BERKS COUNTY
Enlargement
READING
ARCHERY
CLUB
Church Road
Oregon Road
New Holland Road
Nolde Forest EEC Lane
Ledgerock Road
Hickory Road
Freemansville Road
Deer Hill Road
Meadow Glen Lane
Welsh Road
ANGELICA
To Reading, 3.8 Mi.
To Mohnton, 1.2 Mi.
Pipeline
Sawmill
Private Residence
Forester's Bridge
Historic Stone Bridge
Mansion
C.H. McConnell Environmental Education Classroom
Chickadee Nature Discovery Area
Authorized Vehicles Only
Rock Outcrop
Water Tower
Kissinger Bridge
Springs of Punches Run
Fire Gate #3
Fire Gate #4
Fire Gate #5
Painted Turtle Pond
North Pond
Park Office
Blue Symbols Mean ADA Accessible
Environmental Education Classroom
Historic Site
Information Kiosk
Teaching Station
Modern Restrooms
Non-flush Restrooms
Picnicking
Hiking Trail
Paved Trail
Cross-Country Skiing Recommended
Unpaved Road
One-way Road
Gate
Electric Vehicle Charging Station
Parking ADA Accessible
Parking Paved
Parking Unpaved
State Park No Hunting
CONTOURS ARE ON 40 FT. INTERVALS
CONTOURS ARE ON 20 FT. INTERVALS
¾ KILOMETER
½ MILE
Rev. 5/10/22

A single white pine

A Note on the Type

This book is typeset in Palatino, an old-style serif typeface designed by Hermann Zapf, initially released in 1949. Named after the 16th-century Italian master of calligraphy Giambattista Palatino, Palatino is based on the humanist types of the Italian Renaissance, which mirror the letters formed by a broad nib pen reflecting Zapf's expertise as a calligrapher.

Flight Pattern,

Powder Puff Derby, 1948